IMAGES
of America

PORT CHARLOTTE

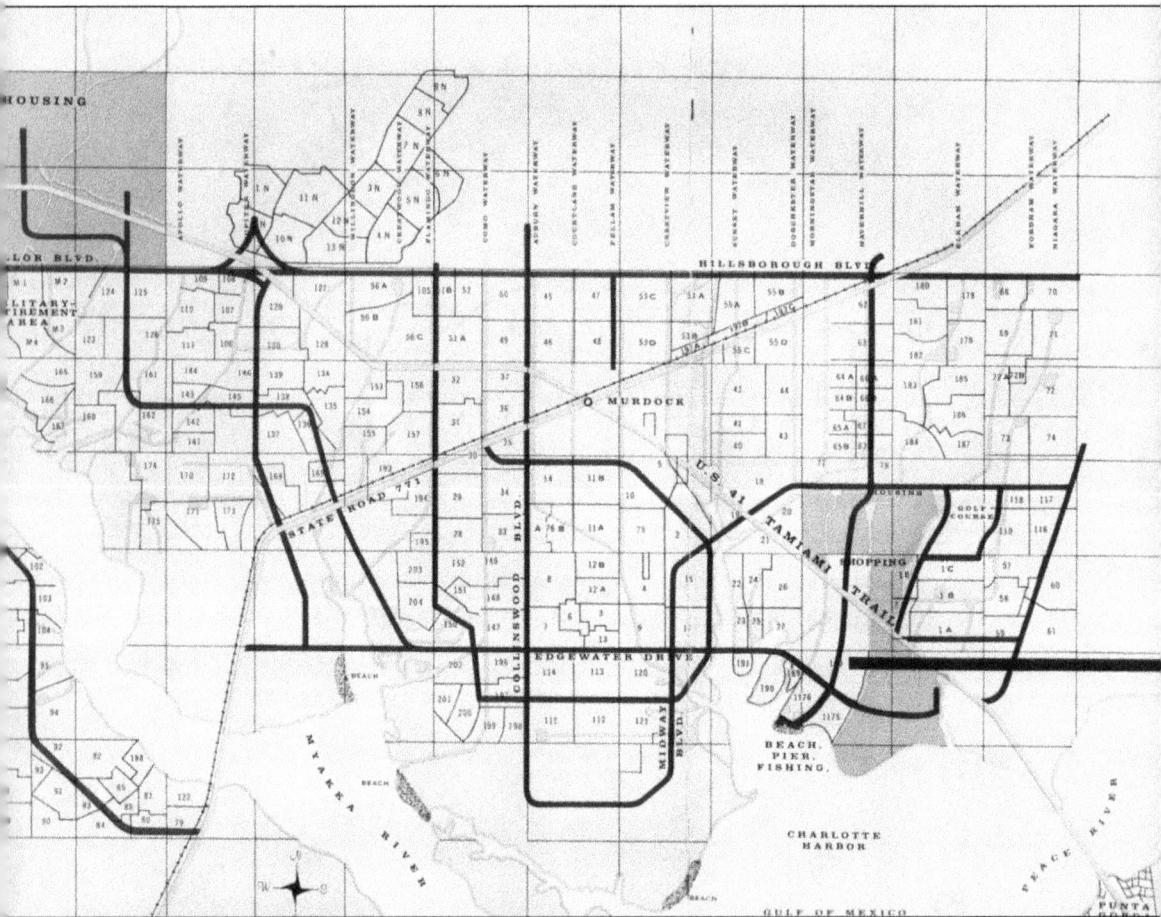

This map appeared in brochures advertising the development of Port Charlotte in the 1960s. Brochures were distributed nationwide in an effort to sell lots and houses to middle-income retirees. Port Charlotte was one of several successful community developments undertaken by Mackle Brothers Construction and General Development Corporation. Other developments in the state of Florida included Vero Beach, Pompano Beach, Lewis Island in St. Petersburg, and Westwood Lake in Miami. (Courtesy of Carolyn Depenbrock.)

ON THE COVER: Port Charlotte "U" was begun in the early 1960s when retirees were flocking to the area and suddenly found they had little to do besides fish, play in the sun, and tend to their new homes. Here an outdoor painting class attracts residents dressed for the subtropical climate. (Courtesy of Charlotte County Historical Center.)

IMAGES
of America

PORT CHARLOTTE

Roxann Read

ARCADIA
PUBLISHING

Published by Arcadia Publishing
Charleston SC, Chicago IL, Portsmouth NH, San Francisco CA

Library of Congress Control Number: 2009921314

For all general information contact Arcadia Publishing at:
Telephone 843-853-2070
Fax 843-853-0044
E-mail sales@arcadiapublishing.com
For customer service and orders:
Toll-Free 1-888-313-2665

Visit us on the Internet at www.arcadiapublishing.com

*To my family; your support has enabled me
to accomplish much in my life.*

CONTENTS

ACKNOWLEDGMENTS

Many, many people have been instrumental in allowing me to tell the story of the Port Charlotte area. Linda Coleman and the staff and volunteers at the Charlotte County Historical Center have been very gracious in letting me spend hours digging through their files. I have examined the works of Lindsey Williams and the late U. S. Cleveland. I am indebted to U. S. Cleveland's indexing of their work, which saved me hours of time. Donna Barrett and Chris Gover of the Cultural Center were extremely helpful in allowing me access to their historical collection. Frank E. Mackle III was very gracious in allowing me to meet with him and pour over his wonderfully well-cataloged collection of historical materials. Others who provided pictures, stories, help, and support are Carolyn Depenbrock, Dee Hawkins and Dave Mahon with Charlotte County Fire and EMS, Lee Stein with Charlotte Symphony, Connie Holmes at Charlotte Harbor School, Port Charlotte High School, Monte Matarese and Tara Prince with Charlotte County mapping division, Mary Behling at Trinity Methodist Church, Bevin Gallo and Melissa Sharrett with Peace River Hospital, Fran Halloran with Charlotte County School District, Diane Nice with Charlotte County Commission Minutes office, Joan Ehrman, Patti Curtis, and Norma Copeland. I would like to thank Steven Ellis and Lindsey Williams, who agreed to proofread the manuscript for accuracy.

This book barely scratches the surface of the history of the Port Charlotte area. I have only been able to capture the highlights here, and in some instances, entire stories have been left out altogether. I would refer the reader to the extensive body of historical information captured in the *Our Fascinating Past* book series by Lindsey Williams and U. S. Cleveland and also to the Charlotte County Historical Center for more information. Finally, I am personally indebted to Gary Mormino (a fellow Florida transplant from Southern Illinois) and Tom Scott (a native Floridian), who have both helped me understand the unique culture of Charlotte County.

INTRODUCTION

Port Charlotte began as a single-family development project for middle-income, factory worker retirees. Though it was once a vast cattle ranch owned by A. C. Frizzell, he sold his 80,000 acres for $3.6 million in 1954 and essentially retired himself. Mackle Brothers Construction and the General Development Corporation used state-of-the-art planning tools to construct a vast city, complete with shopping centers, golf courses, parks, sewer and electric grids and, of course, thousands of single-family homes on small lots. Brochures and salesmen promoted the development all over the United States and ultimately all over the world. Lots in Port Charlotte continue to be owned by people from a variety of countries, and the area has one of the highest retiree populations in the United States. Developments like Port Charlotte sprang up all over Florida in the mid-1950s as middle-income, post–World War II retirees looked for affordable, warm places to live after their working days were over. Port Charlotte is unique in that it was planned to be a city but never became one as most other Mackle developments did. North Port, originally developed as part of Port Charlotte, incorporated in 1959. Gary Mormino, in his book *Land of Sunshine, State of Dreams*, describes the commission form of government as effective for rural communities but not as effective for urban/suburban communities. Port Charlotte was planned as a suburban community, and indeed is one, but still struggles with the rural (and Northern) influences of its inhabitants.

Over the last 50 years, Port Charlotte has experienced unprecedented growth, which has caused concern for its native sons and daughters as they have watched the pine forests and cattle-grazing land that they once knew be swallowed up by modern development. U.S. 41 was a two-lane road in 1954, as can be seen in many of the pictures on the following pages. It is now a major commercial corridor, six lanes through Port Charlotte and eight lanes at many major intersections. From January through April, the height of the "season" as it is called when Northerners winter in Port Charlotte, traffic can be congested even with eight lanes. Commercial businesses developed along U.S. 41 in the typical 1950s and 1960s "strip commercial" style. This pattern of commercial development lingers in Port Charlotte. The devastation of Hurricane Charley in 2004 allowed some modernization of commercial development to occur, but the sheer magnitude of existing strip development has hardly been renovated.

The early pictures of Charlotte Harbor indicate a sense of community in the faces of 80 years ago. With the development of Port Charlotte, people from many different places came together to form a new life that included friends, recreation, and retirement. This new community memorialized its events more in newspaper articles than pictures it seems. Most of the pictures I was able to acquire for inclusion in the book have been aerial photographs or pictures that came from advertising brochures. It seems to suggest that Port Charlotte natives were so shocked by the rapid development that they processed it with the use of aerial photography and let the advertising brochures tell the story of development.

For purposes of this project, I defined Port Charlotte as the region between the Myakka and Peace Rivers. For this reason, photographs of areas such as Rotonda, Englewood, and Punta Gorda were excluded. Charlotte County has a large number of unincorporated neighborhoods, each with a distinctive flavor and culture. Because of this, Port Charlotte exists as a community within a community. I hope this book will enlighten those who read it about the area, and maybe they, too, will better understand it, as I have.

One

1900–1950

This is Charlotte Harbor as it appeared in the 1920s. The Calusa, Timucua, and Seminole tribes had inhabited Charlotte Harbor for hundreds of years and continued their subtropical lifestyle into the 1700s in spite of European exploration. Juan Ponce de Leon landed in Charlotte Harbor in 1513 after petitioning the king of Spain to allow him to explore the area north of Cuba. He landed six days after Easter on the northeast coast of Florida and named the area "La Florida," meaning flowery in Spanish. In 1539, Hernando de Soto is believed to have landed at Charlotte Harbor and began his own exploration of the southeastern United States. In 1567, Pedro Menendez D'Aviles established a mission-fort in Charlotte Harbor (then named San Carlos Bay). Between 1763 and 1783, the British occupied Florida and designated Charlotte Harbor as an American Indian reservation. (Courtesy of Charlotte County Historical Center.)

The first bridge connecting Charlotte Harbor to Punta Gorda was proposed by DeSoto County commissioners John Hagan and William Whitten. Travel across the harbor previously had always been by boat. A special taxing district was created to fund construction of the bridge, which began in 1916. Though it was originally planned as a steel bridge, scarcity of materials during World War I forced a change to a new construction material that involved steel and reinforced concrete. After a halt in construction because of the war, Whitten supplied his own money to complete the 14-foot-wide bridge, dedicated on July 4, 1921. He and John Hagan rode in the first car to cross the bridge, a Model T Ford. The speed limit was 15 miles per hour. (Both courtesy of Charlotte County Historical Center.)

Trinity United Methodist Church was organized in 1873 as Charlotte Harbor's first church with W. P. McEwen as pastor. By 1890, the church was enlarged to accommodate a growing congregation. However, the 1910 hurricane destroyed the second building. This picture, taken August 10, 1924, is of the third church building, badly damaged in the 1926 hurricane. The fourth and present building was constructed in 1949. (Courtesy of Trinity United Methodist Church.)

The picture here was taken by Irving Oxenham and is the 1970 Thanksgiving picnic crew. Those identified are Sam Patton, Arba Snow, Austin Miller, Wesley Vickers, and Larry Loveday. Picnics and "basket lunches" have a long tradition at Trinity, dating back to its beginnings. The church also has a rich history of working together to rebuild and maintain its church buildings. (Courtesy of Trinity United Methodist Church.)

RECORD OF BAPTIZED CHILDREN

Family Name	Christian Name	Father's Name	Mother's Name	Date of Birth	Place of Birth
Roberts	David Frances	F. Curtis	Katie		Charlotte Harbor
Willis	Albert Melvin Jr.	Albert M.	Joyce Knight		" "
Willis	David DeCosta	Elwood	Lillian DeCosta		" "
Hall	Janice Elaine	Murry	Margaret Vickard		" "
Hall	Calvin Murry	Murry	Margaret Vickard	1/26/43	" "
Simpson	Donald Lee	Alton Parker	Estelle E.	2/14/46	Charlotte Harb
Willis	Bettie Joyce	Albert M.	Joyce	8/30/45	" "
Willis	Shelia Lynn	Albert Melvin Jr.	Arnelle Elizabeth	1-16-54	Atlanta Ga
Willis	Sharon Lee	"	"	"	"
Knight Jr.	Thomas Lemuel	Thos. S. Knight	Helen Theresa	9-13-54	Punta Gorda
Workman	Michael Ray	Donald Ray Workman	Hazel Odum	6-15-56	
Rifenburg	James Jerry	James J	Mary J	8-27-47	Titusville Fla
Rifenburg	Keith Eugene	"	"	9-19-48	"
Rifenburg	Lynn Marie	"	"	7-14-49	"

The church building doubled as a school in the 1800s. "Hickory Bluff," as Charlotte Harbor was then called, was part of Manatee County. Parents paid tuition for their children's attendance, and the Manatee County School Board paid $1 per child per term to supplement the $15–20 monthly salary paid to the teacher. Joel Knight, founder of Hickory Bluff (named for the hickory trees there), was the first to be buried in the church's cemetery. The image above is one of the records of baptized children at the church. The image at right is a letter from Pastor J. M. Belt of Nocatee to a Trinity church member who had requested a letter of transfer to her new church. (Both courtesy of Trinity United Methodist Church.)

Nocatee Fla
1920

Dear Miss Dick,

Your request at hand—enclosed find your church letter—I do trust you will be able to get your certificate. If I can in any way help you to get it you may command me. We are all well and trust that this will find you all the same. Give my regards to your mother and grandparents. May God bless and help you.

Your Pastor,

J. M. Belt

This service station was located on Bayshore Drive (once part of U.S. 41) in Charlotte Harbor. The Tamiami Trail, which was finished in 1928 and runs from Tampa to Miami, was originally a wilderness path and progressed to a two-lane road lined with stores, gas stations, and camps for "tin-can" tourists, winter residents who came from the Northern states to escape the cold weather. (Courtesy of Charlotte County Historical Center.)

Mott Willis operated the general store located at the corner of Bayshore Drive and Sibley Bay Street in Charlotte Harbor. He bought the building plus two lots in 1912 for $650. The building was the site of the first general store, post office, and cattle dock. The dock was built during the Civil War by Joel Knight in 1862. (Courtesy of Charlotte County Historical Center.)

Mott Willis was a fisherman whose main business was gathering oysters. He also delivered mail to the outer islands and provided ferry service to Punta Gorda. In 1772, Bernard Romans had surveyed San Carlos Bay for Britain and renamed the estuary Charlotte for England's queen. (Courtesy of Charlotte County Historical Center.)

The United States gained possession of Florida in 1819. During the Civil War, Union ships blockaded Charlotte Harbor. In 1862, a cattle dock was built at Charlotte Harbor, which was then known as Live Oak Point. Joel Knight drove his cattle to the dock via a trail that later became U.S. 41. Ziba King brought his cattle to the dock via an old American Indian trail that is now called King's Highway. The cattle were shipped to Cuba and also supplied to the Confederate army during the Civil War. (Courtesy of Charlotte County Historical Center.)

A free public fish fry was held on July 4, 1921, as part of the dedication ceremony for the first bridge across Charlotte Harbor. Approximately 6,000 people attended. The bridge was originally designed for horse-and-buggy traffic. The concrete mix used to build the bridge included saltwater from the harbor. The use of saltwater in the concrete mix led to rapid deterioration of the bridge. (Courtesy of Charlotte County Historical Center.)

Work on a three-lane bridge began in December 1929. Promoted by Barron Collier, the second Charlotte Harbor bridge cost $1 million. Another free public fish fry was held, and approximately 15,000 people attended the July 4, 1931, dedication ceremony. This picture shows the 60-foot-tall weather tower, from which storm signals and hurricane flags were displayed until 1960. (Courtesy of Charlotte County Historical Center.)

The discovery of phosphate in the Peace River in 1887 sparked a booming phosphate industry. The *Mary Blue* was a paddle-wheel tugboat that towed phosphate barges down the river to Punta Gorda. The phosphate was loaded onto ships, which carried it to the East Coast for shipping to Europe and Japan. In 1904, phosphate shipped through Punta Gorda totaled 81,650 tons. (Courtesy of Charlotte County Historical Center.)

The Charlotte Harbor commercial fishing industry was one of the largest operations in Florida during the first half of the 20th century. "Run boats" regularly brought ice and supplies from the Punta Gorda Ice Plant to preserve the fish catch. Iced fish were loaded onto the run boat and then brought to Punta Gorda for processing and shipping to New York, Philadelphia, and Chicago. (Courtesy of Charlotte County Historical Center.)

The Willis Fish Cabin at Bull Bay was built in the mid-1920s by Claude Willis, an oysterman from Charlotte Harbor. It allowed commercial fishermen to stay at the fishing grounds Monday through Saturday. The cabin could be lifted off its pilings and moved to more abundant fishing grounds, if needed. The fish cabin is listed on the National Register of Historic Places. (Courtesy of Charlotte County Historical Center.)

Icehouses were stilt houses in the water where fish catches were stored until the return of the run boat, which transported the fish back to the mainland fish houses. An open deck served as a loading area for 300-pound cakes of ice and fish catches. The fish were iced and stored in a room with double-thick cypress walls. (Courtesy of Charlotte County Historical Center.)

This picture shows Elmer Powell's fish crew in 1942. From left to right are Austin Powell, Charlie Griggs, and Jerry Powell. In the early 1900s, nearly 300 people worked in the commercial fishing industry in Charlotte Harbor. (Courtesy of Charlotte County Historical Center.)

This picture shows Sammy Holmes (left) and Andrew Owen (right), who worked for Punta Gorda Fish Company in 1946. In 1886, the railroad was completed to Long Dock, a 4,200-foot dock built to deep water where steamships could tie up to directly receive passengers and freight transferred from rail lines. This was located about a mile west of present-day Fisherman's Village. Several fish companies including the Punta Gorda Fish Company, established in 1897, occupied space at Old Long Dock. (Courtesy of Charlotte County Historical Center.)

A new railroad dock located at the foot of King Street in Punta Gorda was built in 1897, and the fish companies relocated from Old Long Dock to the King Street dock, where they stayed until a fire in 1915 destroyed nearly all the fish houses. The Punta Gorda Fish Company was one of the few fish companies to survive the fire and continued to operate until 1977. (Courtesy of Charlotte County Historical Center.)

The Hotel Punta Gorda (later Hotel Charlotte Harbor) can be seen in the background. Hotel guests included Pres. Theodore Roosevelt, Thomas Edison, and Henry Ford. (Courtesy of Charlotte County Historical Center.)

Home of the Riggs Family in Charlotte Harbor

Some of the families of Charlotte Harbor are seen in these pictures. The above picture shows the John and Virginia Riggs family at their home on Laura Street in the early 1900s. John Riggs, a commercial fisherman, had moved his family here from North Carolina. The picture below shows the home of Lloyd and Maud Mauck. Maud Mauck was secretary to Sallie Jones, one of the original 21 teachers at Charlotte High School. Sallie graduated from Punta Gorda High in 1913 and completed a six-week training course to teach primary grades. She created the first school lunchrooms and instituted the policy that all teachers needed to be professionally certified. She was elected superintendent in 1937 and served for 16 years, making her the longest serving Charlotte County superintendent. (Both courtesy of Charlotte County Historical Center.)

Nathan DeCoster is the bearded man in the center, shown here with his grandchildren in 1910. He was a Union soldier who was stationed at Fort Myers during the Civil War. After the war, DeCoster moved to Charlotte Harbor. He purchased 160 acres and platted Harbor View. He planted half the acreage in citrus to provide extra income for retirees and winter visitors. (Courtesy of Charlotte County Historical Center.)

Mr. Hiram. Curry's. Resident. & Oranges Grove,
Harbour - View. Fla.

The Hiram Curry residence is shown in this picture. After the Civil War, the village at Live Oak Point had expanded to Hickory Bluff and Harbor View. When John Bartholf was appointed postmaster at Hickory Bluff in 1876, he named the post office Charlotte Harbor to describe the territory. (Courtesy of Charlotte County Historical Center.)

Hiram Curry was Maude Mauck's grandfather. Curry tended the lighthouse near the Punta Gorda long dock at the terminal of the Florida Southern Railway from 1896 to 1899. On April 20, 1921, the state legislature approved the division of DeSoto County into five counties: DeSoto, Glades, Hardee, Highlands, and Charlotte, as it was named by the people who inhabited the county at the time. (Courtesy of Charlotte County Historical Center.)

The *Punta Gorda Herald* had offered a $10 prize for the winning name. Names suggested were Charlotte, Punta Gorda, Roosevelt, Fairweather, Good Health, Homeland, Justice, Pineapple, Fruitland, Harbor, Avalon, Beulah, Palm, Avocado, Daisy, Mullet, Tarpon, and Tourist. Charlotte was chosen with 199 votes out of the 317 votes that were cast. (Courtesy of Charlotte County Historical Center.)

By 1890, Harbor View had its own school. In 1911, enrollment was 42. The families of students provided room and board to the teachers, and fishermen would row the teachers across the harbor to and from school. Both schools were abandoned when Charlotte Harbor School, seen above, was built in 1917. Its original location was at the corner of U.S. 41 and Kings Highway, the site of the Schoolhouse Square Plaza. Teachers there taught first through eighth grades. High school students were transported to Punta Gorda High School by boat. The below picture from 1939 shows the Bermont schoolhouse and school bus. The only person identified in this picture is Elmer Friday, who is fourth from the left on the ground. (Both courtesy of Charlotte County Historical Center.)

The Forrest Nelson family is seen here. Forrest Nelson came to Port Charlotte in 1907 with his parents and siblings to aid in improving his mother's poor health. They settled in Harbor View. Forrest's father, John Nelson, ran cattle, harvested oranges, and built a one-room schoolhouse for his eight children and the neighbors' children. (Courtesy of the Charlotte County Historical Center.)

Forrest, the oldest child, became a horticulturist who worked for Barron Collier. In 1930, he bought 180 acres in Murdock for $600 where he built a home at the end of a dirt road that later became Forrest Nelson Boulevard. The picture shows Forrest holding the orchid plants that he grew. (Courtesy of Charlotte County Historical Center.)

This picture shows an African American "leased" convict hauling barrels of sap at a turpentine camp at the dawn of the 20th century. One of the largest camps was located in Southland, later El Jobe-an. When harsh treatment resulted in death, workers were buried in the camp cemetery or along the railroad tracks. The Florida Legislature outlawed the leasing of convicts in 1923. (Courtesy of Charlotte County Historical Center.)

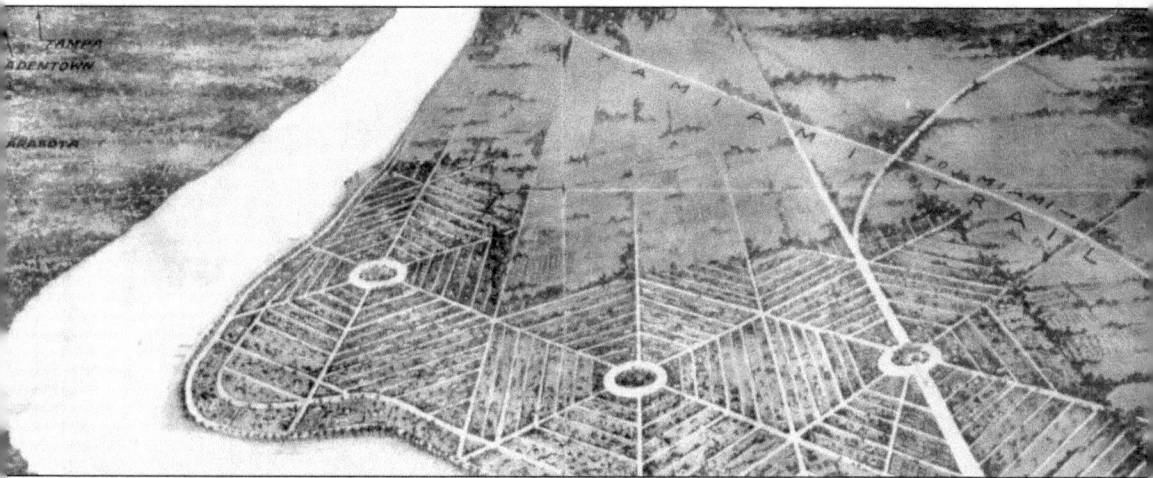

Joel Bean had been somewhat successful in building coastal towns in Massachusetts. He formed the Boston-Florida Realty Trust and paid $62,141 for 1,071 acres in "Southland" in 1923. He planned six hexagonal communities, each to have a plaza in the center surrounded by a 100-foot-wide boulevard. The communities were to be connected with 80-foot-wide thoroughfares. (Courtesy of Charlotte County Historical Center.)

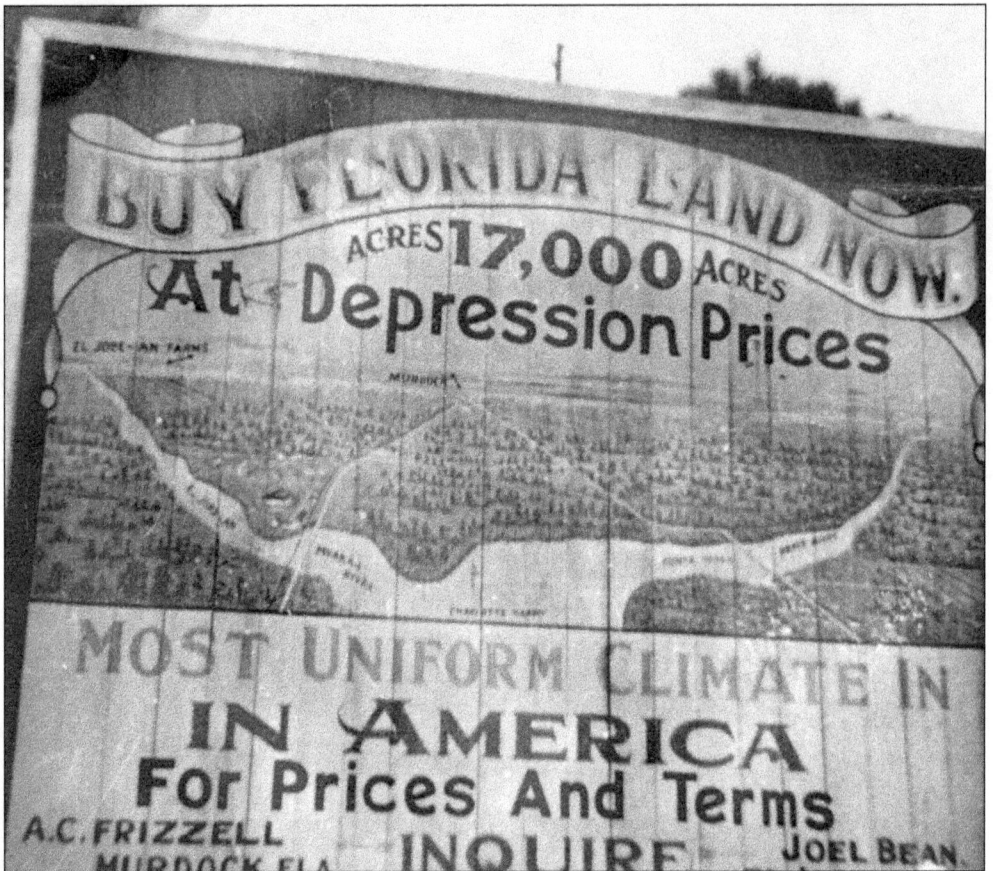

Bean renamed the area El Jobe-an to give the place an exotic appeal. Northerners began to buy the 50-by-100-foot lots sight-unseen with a small down payment. Bean then constructed a small cottage, hotel, and a combination store, post office, and home. Bean enlarged the hotel to accommodate visitors, such as MGM movie crews who filmed *Tarzan* serials at the site. The stock market crash of 1929 forced landowners to abandon the mortgages on the lots, and the Boston-Florida Realty Trust folded. When Joel Bean died at the cottage in El Jobean (note the current spelling) in 1942, neighbors took up a collection to pay his funeral expenses. (Both courtesy of Charlotte County Historical Center.)

Two

MURDOCK

This photograph of the back of the Murdock Railroad Station was taken around 1915. The Charlotte Harbor and Northern Railroad had been completed to Murdock, opening up the pine forests for exploitation by the naval stores industry. The work was largely done through forced labor by leased convicts or poor African Americans. It is reported that workers at the turpentine camps in Florida were treated harshly. They were paid $1 a day and suffered beatings at times. The workers collected resin from the pine trees using a technique that eventually killed the trees. The collected resin was then converted into turpentine and shipped out of the Murdock station. Large turpentine camps were located throughout Charlotte County at places called Mars, Acline, Evaland, Southland, Pineland, and Vineland. Convicts were also leased from the DeSoto County jail to clear right-of-way and build a grade through the swamp for the railroad. (Courtesy of Charlotte County Historical Center.)

In 1907, the Charlotte Harbor and Northern Railroad (CH&N) completed its line to Murdock. The American Agricultural Chemical Company financed the railroad construction in order to carry phosphate from the Peace River to a loading dock at Boca Grande. The railroad provided housing for the Irish construction workers. CH&N also built a loading dock for a turpentine camp located at the intersection of the railroad tracks and a sand trail that ran between Charlotte Harbor and Englewood. Part of the trail is now U.S. 41. J. B. Moody built a store at this intersection and established a post office there in 1908. Smaller train depots were built at El Jobean, Cleveland, Acline, Placida, and McCall. (Both courtesy of Charlotte County Historical Center.)

John Murdock, a real estate salesman from Chicago, bought strips of land along the railroad rights-of-way and gave the land to the railroad company, who in turn constructed a two-story depot and telegraph office and renamed the station Murdock. He began negotiating with speculators to buy land in Florida in 1910. It is said his first agreement involved offering farm-lot packages to buyers for $10 down and $10 a month. He then sold 10 acres of land to his father-in-law before he had obtained the deed to the property. He eventually acquired two townships, 80 acres near the railroad station, and Moody's store with clear title. (Both courtesy of Charlotte County Historical Center.)

Murdock built a two-story headquarters and hotel for prospective buyers that served as a sales office, home, school, church, dining hall, and living quarters for his employees. His plan was to start a farm colony, and he sold the plots sight-unseen to Northern buyers on land contracts from the Murdock Land Company. Murdock, aggravated that the rainy season made farming impossible, petitioned the DeSoto County Commission (Charlotte County had not yet been created) to establish a drainage district. The commission approved, and Murdock was the lowest bidder for the excavation work. Murdock began construction on 20 drainage canals in 1913. One of Murdock's steam shovels was dynamited by an angry landowner. Unfortunately, the canals were too deep and drained the water that was needed for farming. (Both courtesy of Charlotte County Historical Center.)

The entire complex seen in these pictures was located at the present-day site of the Port Charlotte Town Center Mall. A. C. Frizzell, who later bought the property, demolished the hotel and general store after the 1926 hurricane and used the lumber to build four small houses for his employees. He also built a new concrete-block store near the railroad. When he sold his land to General Development Corporation in 1954, he moved the homes and store 1 mile south to the area of Cochran Boulevard and U.S. 41. After his death in 1961, the store became the DeSoto Groves fruit market. The homes were later torn down to extend Cochran Boulevard east. Cochran Boulevard was formerly known as Toledo Blade Boulevard, named for the *Toledo Blade* newspaper in Toledo, Ohio. (Both courtesy of Charlotte County Historical Center.)

When Murdock's farming colony began to fail, he left his family and moved to Jacksonville in 1916. His land was sold for back taxes. A newcomer named Arthur C. Frizzell bought the small general store and 20 acres of pine woods for $600. The picture below is a Frizzell family photograph. It is not known which family member is A. C. He came to Port Charlotte in 1918 as a railroad telegrapher making $68 a month and supplemented his income by starting a small farm behind the station. He was fired after 90 days on the job at the Murdock station. (Courtesy of Charlotte County Historical Center.)

Three

A. C. Frizzell

Arthur C. Frizzell (A. C.) came to Port Charlotte in 1918 from Alabama with his wife, Patti. He worked as a railroad telegrapher and station agent at the Murdock railroad depot. They started a small farm behind the station to provide additional income. With the proceeds from the farm, they bought a small general store at Murdock and 20 acres of pine woods located at a place called Mars, which was a railroad loading dock. A. C. also began a turpentine operation there. Mars was north of Peachland Boulevard and west of Kings Highway. He continued to buy land at 50¢ an acre from big companies that did not want to pay taxes on the land because they had exhausted the pine trees' resin yield. Out of the stumps and palmettos that were left, Frizzell was able to manufacture paint thinner, pine tar, and gunpowder. (Courtesy of Charlotte County Historical Center.)

The pictures on the following pages were taken by A. C. Frizzell in 1954 as he prepared to sell his land. The above picture is of the bridge over the Myakka River, and below is a fish house at the foot of a bridge that crosses to what was then called Punta Gorda Beach (known today as Englewood Beach). During the Great Depression, he continued to buy land for 20–30¢ an acre, amassing approximately 80,000 acres that he sold to Yellow Knife Bear Mines, Ltd., a Canadian investment firm, which formed a partnership with the Mackle Brothers Construction Company and later became General Development Corporation. (Both courtesy of Charlotte County Historical Center.)

Frizzell has labeled these pictures "Big Slough." This is possibly in the North Port area. A slough is essentially a swamp or marsh. Frizzell became an apprentice to Patti Standifer, a widow with two children. It is said that she was old enough to be Frizzell's mother. They married in 1913 and came to Florida because of their jobs with the railroad. Patti became a station agent at Gardner, and Frizzell became a station agent at Murdock. They lived in a small house near the Murdock station. Soon after Frizzell began his employment at Murdock, the railroad president came to visit. Frizzell was tending his garden on company time and was promptly fired. (Both courtesy of Charlotte County Historical Center.)

These pictures are of Boar Hammock Slough, possibly in the North Port area. When Frizzell was fired from the railroad, he had managed to save $600, which was enough to buy the general store at Murdock and 20 acres of pine woods. He began a turpentine operation there, using leased convicts to bleed the trees and boil the resin. When the trees died from prolonged bleeding, he had the trees sawed into lumber. With the money that he earned from the initial 20 acres, he bought other patches of trees that the big lumber companies had left in hard-to-reach places for 50¢ an acre. He also bought a small sawmill that could be moved to those hard-to-reach patches, enabling him to cut the lumber cheaply. (Both courtesy of Charlotte County Historical Center.)

These pictures are of a gladiola bulb farm near Burnt Store. The small white specks on the ground are grazing cows. Frizzell planted pasture grass and went into the cattle business, establishing a large herd, hiring cowboys, and building houses for them and their families. James E. Whidden Jr. tended cattle for Frizzell. Whidden's great-grandfather had established a large herd of cattle on 7,000 acres at Deep Creek in 1861. Frizzell paid his employees in money that was good only at his general store in Murdock. The only other store was 8 miles away down a dirt road to Charlotte Harbor. (Both courtesy of Charlotte County Historical Center.)

Frizzell calls the above picture "Little Salt Springs Crevis." Little Salt Springs is located in North Port and is on the National Register of Historic Places. It was originally thought that Little Salt Spring was a shallow freshwater pond, but in the 1950s, divers discovered that it was a true sinkhole, extending down over 200 feet. It has produced the second-oldest dated artifact ever found in the southeastern United States, a wooden stake thought to be 12,000 years old. Little Salt Spring contains some of the oldest cultural remains in Florida. The site has been owned by the University of Miami since 1982. The below picture is the pines in an area Frizzell called "North Joshlin." (Both courtesy of Charlotte County Historical Center.)

Frizzell labeled these areas "North Joshlin." When Frizzell cut the lumber on his land, it left tree stumps that were loaded with resin. He soon realized that the stumps were valuable, so he bought a bulldozer to root them out and sell them to the Hercules Powder Company in Jacksonville. The company processed the stumps into paint thinner, pine tar, and gunpowder. At that time, the federal government was paying farmers to improve the soil, so after Frizzell removed the stumps, he scraped off the palmettos and planted Bahia pasture grass. He then bought some cattle and hired cowboys. (Both courtesy of Charlotte County Historical Center.)

These pictures are of Alligator Bay in an area Frizzell called "Jorden pasture." Alligator Bay is the water body adjacent to the Port Charlotte Beach Complex. At one time, Frizzell owned two lumberyards in Punta Gorda and several car dealerships along with the 80,000 acres. When he sold his land to Yellowknife Bear Mines, he kept 40 acres in Murdock in the area where the Days Inn is located, near Cochran Boulevard and U.S. 41. After he sold the land to Yellowknife, he built a house on the 40 acres in Murdock. (Both courtesy of Charlotte County Historical Center.)

The above picture is called "Murdock house." This could be a house that John Murdock occupied at one time. It is unknown where the house was located on Frizzell's property. The picture below is labeled "looking south from U.S. 41, Dow canal, south of Brantley Place." There is a Dow Waterway and a Dow Road in the area where some of the first housing development occurred in the 1950s. It is unknown if this is an early picture of Dow Waterway. This could be a canal dug by John Murdock. Early canals appear to have originally been drainage ditches that were expanded into canals to provide dry land suitable for building construction. (Both courtesy of Charlotte County Historical Center.)

This picture shows the intersection of U.S. 41 and State Route 776. The railroad tracks are now Veterans Parkway. The railroad depot is in the lower right corner. U.S. 41 is the white strip in the lower right corner. The old DeSoto Groves store can be seen in this picture, across the railroad tracks from the small houses. (Courtesy of Charlotte County Historical Center.)

These are the loading pens at the railroad depot at Murdock. The railroad cars can also be seen in the top picture in the lower right corner. The old DeSoto Groves store can also be seen in the top picture in the white circle on the right side of the picture. (Courtesy of Charlotte County Historical Center.)

Four

THE BIRTH OF
"PORT CHARLOTTE"

Welcome to PORT CHARLOTTE

America's most talked about planned home community

We welcome you as a future property owner at Port Charlotte, Florida's exciting new home community on the unspoiled southwest coast of the Sunshine State. We believe you have made a wise decision, and we are certain that as time passes you will be even more proud of your foresight in taking this important step for your future.

As you can readily see from the actual photographs in this brochure, your homesite is part of an active, growing Florida home community. More than 1000 homes have already been built and are being lived in . . . others are being completed every day. Two hundred and fifty miles of roads and streets have been graded and prepared for paving . . . 50 miles have actually been paved, and work is continuing at an average of 5 miles per week.

In addition to enjoying the natural advantages that Port Charlotte offers, such as the beautiful setting, with 40 miles of picturesque waterfront, high, dry, fertile land, excellent fishing, boating, swimming and shopping facilities . . . other extra facilities for the pleasure and convenience of Port Charlotte property owners have been completed. These include a wide, sandy bathing beach, a 450 ft. fishing pier, Civic Center building, shuffleboard courts, horseshoe pits, baseball diamond, picnic area (complete with barbecue grill) and refreshment stand on the beach. There is also an existing shopping area with a supermarket, service station, hardware store, barber shop, TV and radio repair shop.

All these have been built and are being used today.

But that's not all! Extra facilities are already planned for the future, such as an 18 hole championship golf course (9 holes now under construction) and a community Yacht Club.

As part of a master plan, other home communities are being built at Port Charlotte . . . each to have its own community facilities, its own shopping center, playground, parks, etc.

All this is yours now as a property owner at Port Charlotte. Just compare the many extras that have actually been built and are in use . . . compare the location . . . compare the cost with any other community anywhere, and we're sure you'll be even more pleased that you selected Port Charlotte.

$10 down $10 a month
FOR A BIG 80' x 125' HOMESITE

The advertisements on this page and the following page appeared in brochures advertising Port Charlotte, a retirement community planned by Mackle Brothers Construction and General Development Corporation. The next several pages will outline the history of the development of Port Charlotte. In 1928, the Chemical Research Corporation was formed. Its business was developing new technological processes and equipment for the oil industry. By 1954, the company's primary investment was in cement and building materials. As the company's business focus changed, the company's name changed to the Florida Canada Corporation. In 1908, Frank Mackle Sr. had launched a construction business in Jacksonville, Florida, and eventually involved his sons, Elliott, Frank Jr., and Robert. Thirty years later, Frank Jr. began building homes in South Florida. By 1954, Mackle Brothers Construction had expanded from its base in Dade County into Broward, Pinellas, Indian River, St. Lucie, and Charlotte Counties. (Courtesy of Carolyn Depenbrock.)

This modern Community Center has facilities for activities of all kinds and is the popular meeting place for residents and visitors.

The Port Charlotte Post Office, now completed, maintains full postal service including daily mail delivery to your door.

PORT CHARLOTTE IS A "READY-NOW" COMMUNITY WITH ALL FACILITIES FOR GRACIOUS LIVING

As Port Charlotte has grown and prospered, facilities have kept pace . . . and will continue, as outlined in the Master Plan. The newest addition is the PORT CHARLOTTE BANK, providing full banking service for your convenience. Thus, you don't have to wonder what this community may be like in the future . . . you *know* it will become an even finer place for your Re-new-ment as the years pass.

A modern supermarket located in one of Port Charlotte's three shopping centers.

The Mackle Brothers and Florida Canada Corporation entered into a 50/50 partnership that was called Port Charlotte, Inc. Florida Canada's primary business then switched to financier of the Mackle partnership. (Courtesy of Charlotte County Historical Center.)

HERE'S HOW WE BUILD AT *Port Charlotte*

The use of 100%-Union labor, quality workmanship and excellence of materials to build the best homes in the finest locations at the lowest possible cost has become a hallmark of Mackle-built homes. The Mackle Company is the largest builder and developer in the South and the ninth largest builder of homes in the Nation. Building is our business. The savings created by our purchasing power is passed on to you.

HERE'S WHAT GOES INTO YOUR HOME AT PORT CHARLOTTE:

- Masonry construction.
- Walls furred and plastered.
- Reinforced concrete floors with Goldseal tile covering.
- Glass jalousie windows and doors with aluminum frames and screens.
- Large storage and utility rooms.
- Plumbing fixtures Richmond or equal.
- GE hot water heaters with 10-year warranty.
- Factory-made kitchen cabinets.
- Outlets installed for electric stoves and refrigerators.
- Several electric outlets in each room.
- Gas radiation heater installed.
- Aluminum screening on porches.
- Front and side lawns sprig planted.
- Sanitary sewer system.
- Streets graded and paved.
- Combination tubs and showers.

**No municipal taxes...No assessments for improvements
No state income taxes**

A typical community scene (Key Biscayne—Built by Mackle Company)

Florida Canada's subsidiary, Florida West Coast Land, held options on approximately 80,000 acres that had been purchased from A. C. Frizzell at $43 an acre. The land in Charlotte County was dry, had good subsoil, and was cheaper because it was not adjacent to an already developed major city center like Fort Myers or Venice. (Courtesy of Frank E. Mackle III.)

Here are three reservation coupons for Port Charlotte homesites. Remember, $10 down and $10 a month buys a king size 80 x 125 ft. lot (full 10,000 square feet).

One of these coupons is for your use—the first step in making your Florida Dream come true. The other two coupons are available for your friends—to give them the opportunity to also enjoy Florida's relaxed way of living at Port Charlotte.

YOUR COUPON

PORT CHARLOTTE DIVISION
GENERAL DEVELOPMENT CORP.
P. O. Box 465, Miami 45, Florida
Dept. B01

Please reserve .... (fill in number desired) lots (each 80 ft. x 125 ft.) as described in this brochure. I enclose $10.00 payment on each. Rush map showing location. My deposit will be returned promptly and without question if I notify you within 30 days.
(Please print—giving name exactly as you want it on purchase contract)

NAME ....
ADDRESS ....
CITY .... ZONE ...... STATE ......
TELEPHONE NUMBER ....

FOR YOUR FRIENDS

PORT CHARLOTTE DIVISION
GENERAL DEVELOPMENT CORP.
P. O. Box 465, Miami 45, Florida
Dept. B02

Please reserve .... (fill in number desired) lots (each 80 ft. x 125 ft.) as described in this brochure. I enclose $10.00 payment on each. Rush map showing location. My deposit will be returned promptly and without question if I notify you within 30 days.
(Please print—giving name exactly as you want it on purchase contract)

NAME ....
ADDRESS ....
CITY .... ZONE ...... STATE ......
TELEPHONE NUMBER ....

PORT CHARLOTTE DIVISION
GENERAL DEVELOPMENT CORP.
P. O. Box 465, Miami 45, Florida
Dept. B02

Please reserve .... (fill in number desired) lots (each 80 ft. x 125 ft.) as described in this brochure. I enclose $10.00 payment on each. Rush map showing location. My deposit will be returned promptly and without question if I notify you within 30 days.
(Please print—giving name exactly as you want it on purchase contract)

NAME ....
ADDRESS ....
CITY .... ZONE ...... STATE ......
TELEPHONE NUMBER ....

These images are part of a national advertising campaign pitched to middle-income retirees. The first major advertising campaign for "$10 dollars down and $10 a month" was begun in 1957. These images are part of that campaign. The customer would return the coupon along with a $10 bill to reserve a home site. Customers were encouraged to buy more than one lot since the reservation coupons usually came in sets of three. (Both courtesy of Frank E. Mackle III.)

In 1956, the Port Charlotte, Inc., partnership was merged with three other Florida partnerships into one partnership named General Development Corporation. In 1958, the Mackles merged their interest in General Development Corporation into Florida Canada Corporation and took over the management. At this time also, Florida Canada changed its name to General Development Corporation. Port Charlotte was originally a "housing only" development, and sales were very slow at first. Until the 1950s, home builders relied on local advertising and on-site sales to sell new houses. The Mackles started to experiment with a few out-of-state offices to sell house and lot packages. (Both courtesy of Frank E. Mackle III.)

Recreational Facilities

The Mackle Company has selected with care and planned with precision at Port Charlotte. We build more than homes. We build a new way of life. Our experience in building for the retirement field makes recreational facilities such as those shown here an eventual adjunct to each community.

Community Workshop

Public Beach

Community Park

Mineral Springs

These brochures show the amenities of the Port Charlotte development. In late 1954, the Mackles ran an advertisement in the *Saturday Evening Post* to get Northerners interested in buying Florida homes. However, many people indicated that they wanted to purchase a home when they retired, which could be 10 years in the future. So they developed the idea of selling a home site for the future construction of a retirement home by mail order. The Mackles' idea was to sell lots on an installment contract basis using national advertising, brochures, and coupons. When the purchaser had paid the contract in full, the Mackles would deed the home site to the buyer. All roads, utility lines, and other amenities would be in place. It was then the owner's responsibility to build the house. (Both courtesy of Frank E. Mackle III.)

Neighborhood Facilities

The Mackle Company builds complete and planned communities at Port Charlotte. As the community grows, facilities similar to those illustrated here are provided for residents at no cost to the homeowner.

CLINIC

SHOPPING CENTER

VOLUNTEER FIRE DEPARTMENT

WATER WORKS

Advertising then expanded internationally, which resulted in customers from all over the world purchasing lots in Port Charlotte. Soon the mail-order system was replaced by the out-of-state sales office and branch office network created for lot sales. The Florida Canada Annual Report stated that land sales in 1956 totaled $2.6 million. With the mail order campaign in 1957, that total reached $15.5 million. Installment land sales accounted for 70 percent of the Mackles' business in 1957. In 1958, *House and Home Magazine* named the Mackle Company as the number one homebuilder in the nation with 2,504 housing starts. (Both courtesy of Frank E. Mackle III.)

The fabulous story of
PORT CHARLOTTE

HOW *you can stake out your claim to a homesite for retirement, vacation, everyday living or as an investment hedge against inflation in the choice waterfront community . . . . on the growth coast of Florida!*

This picture shows Frank Mackle Sr. (left) and Elliott Mackle (second from left). The gentleman pointing is unidentified, and Bill Gregory is on the right. Gregory was the project manager for the Port Charlotte Development. The newly developed community is visible in the background. (Courtesy of Frank E. Mackle III.)

F.H.A. and V.__
MORTGAGE LOAN

This COMPANY ARRANGES THE FINANCING
FOR MACKLE COMPANY HOUSES THROUGHOUT
THE STATE *of* FLORIDA

PRESENTLY FINANCING
IN ADDITION TO
WESTWOOD LAKE:
ANO BEACH HIGHLANDS, Broward Cou
EWIS ISLAND, St. Petersburg. Pinella County
RT CHARLOTTE, Punta Gorda. Charlotte C

In 1959, the Mackle Brothers expanded the Port Charlotte development from 80,000 acres to 92,700 acres, which included North Port. North Port was originally introduced as North Port Charlotte. Since Port Charlotte was not immediately adjacent to an already existing city, all city amenities needed to be developed as the project expanded. (Courtesy of Frank E. Mackle III.)

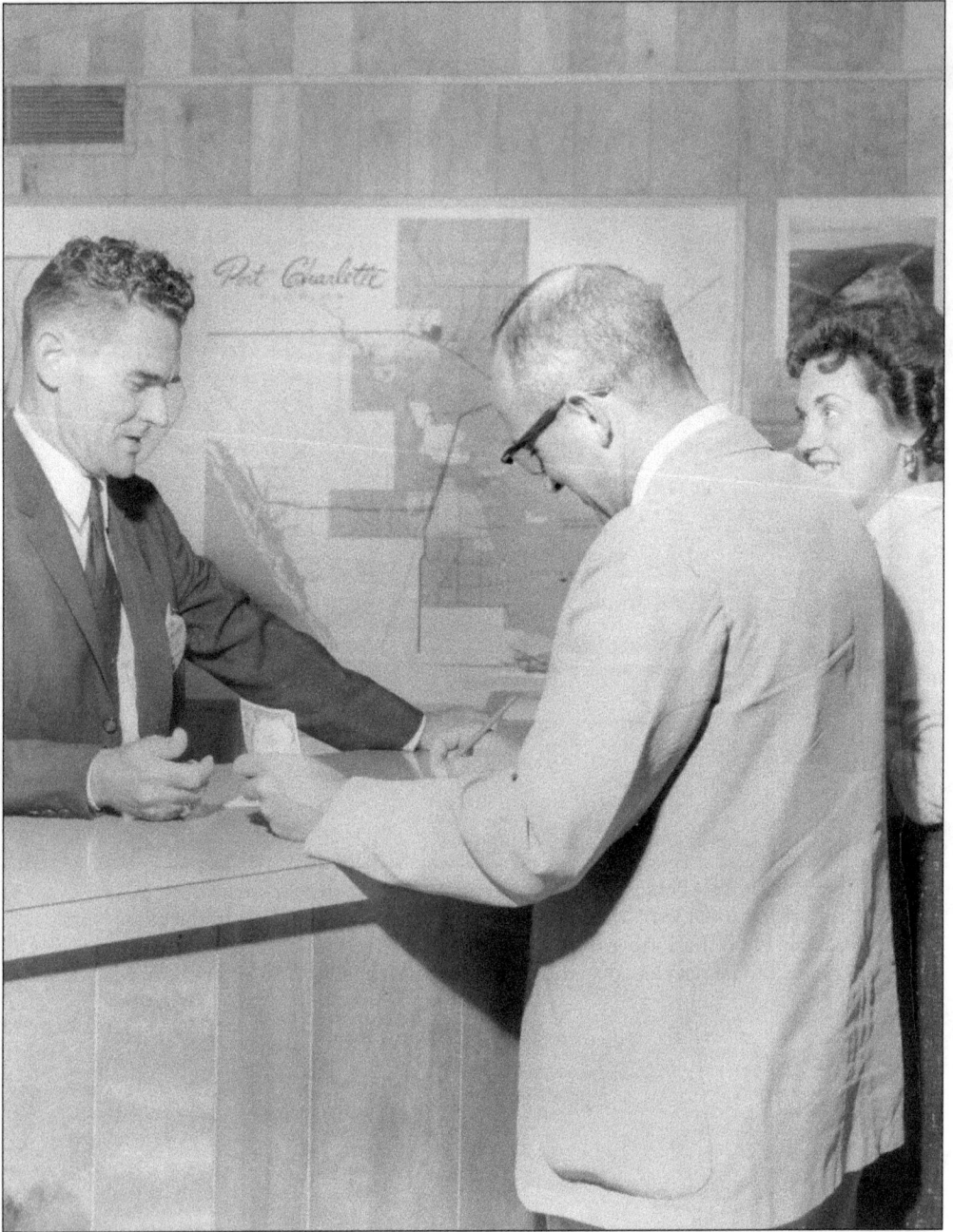

This picture shows a customer making his initial $10 down payment on a lot in Port Charlotte. (Courtesy of Frank E. Mackle III.)

This picture shows Mr. and Mrs. Douglas Read of Toronto, Canada, leaving home in October 1962. They were chosen to represent the 10,000th resident of Port Charlotte and honored at a ceremony at the cultural center. The first installment lot contracts had been written in Port Charlotte in late 1955. An article in the *Miami Daily News* in December 1955 stated that 200 home sites were sold in Port Charlotte in less than a month and that the 80-by-125-foot "inside" lots were selling for $699. (Courtesy of Frank E. Mackle III.)

These illustrations were printed in brochures advertising the different housing types that Mackle Brothers Construction built in Port Charlotte. These typically 800-900-square-foot homes boasted one, two, and three bedrooms with carports, patios, and porches. A variety of housing styles were offered. In planning Port Charlotte, the Mackle Brothers utilized 1960s state-of-the-art city planning tools. Along with single-family retirement homes, they planned and constructed parks, churches, shopping centers, golf courses, boat ramps, roads, and water, sewer, gas, and power lines. Franchised sales offices began to spring up in late 1957. By 1958, there were 26 sales offices in more than 100 northern cities. (Both courtesy of Carolyn Depenbrock.)

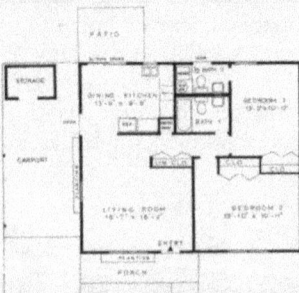

2 BEDROOMS, 1½ BATHS, PATIO, OPEN FRONT PORCH, CARPORT

Two-car carports, one-car garages, two-car garages are optional on all houses. See optional extra list for prices.

CENTURY LINE MODEL 100-A

These pictures show the beginnings of the development at Port Charlotte. The above picture shows U.S. 41 in the foreground with a welcome center at the bottom middle of the picture. A new housing development is shown on the left-hand side of the picture with a lake in the middle of the circle development. The below picture shows the creation of Martin Drive, Gregory Drive, and Waterway Circle with new housing starting in 1957. U.S. 41 is in the foreground with the Peace River at the top of the picture. The Martin Drive exit off of U.S. 41 is shown at the bottom of the picture, and the beginnings of Easy Street are seen as the second exit off of U.S. 41 near the bottom middle of the picture. (Both courtesy of Charlotte County Historical Center.)

The pictures on this page show the development of the area between the Elkcam (on the right) and Fordham (on the left) Waterways. (Elkcam is Mackle spelled backwards.) The above picture is dated 1958; the below picture 1959. The area of trees above has become the home sites in the picture below. U.S. 41 can barely be seen in both pictures, running from left to right near the top of the picture. Along the left side runs Conway Boulevard to its intersection with U.S. 41. The Mackle lighthouse can barely be seen. To the left of Conway is the area that is now the New York section. The below picture is taken from Mallory Avenue looking south. (Both courtesy of Charlotte County Historical Center.)

These pictures are from General Development Corporation's annual reports from 1958 and 1960 describing the Port Charlotte development. Model homes in New York's Grand Central Station and Philadelphia's train station were built to create interest in the development. Franchise offices were established overseas. When a coupon was sent in to GDC headquarters, it was sent out to a local area sales office. The "lead" was given to a local sales representative, who set up a home appointment. The sales rep made an attempt to close a sale on the first visit. If the closing was not achieved, the customer was offered a "sponsored trip." They would be asked to sign a contract and make a small deposit. If they were not satisfied after a personal inspection of Port Charlotte, the contract was cancelled. (Both courtesy of Frank E. Mackle III.)

The picture at left shows the culs-de-sac of Roselle Court on the right and Baldwin Court on the left. The below picture shows the continued development in the area between Elkcam and Fordham Waterways. This view is from Beverly Avenue looking south. The beginnings of Augusta Avenue can be seen at the bottom of the picture. St. Charles Borremeo Church had not yet been built at Augusta Avenue and Easy Street (rectangular lot at the bottom right). (Both courtesy of Charlotte County Historical Center.)

Potential buyers and their spouses would come to Port Charlotte for the weekend as part of a charter group on a GDC-sponsored trip. The group gathered at bus or train terminals on Thursday or Friday afternoons for the trip to Port Charlotte. Later on, chartered airplanes were involved. On the weekend vacation, the group would be shown the model homes and the local area. There were also dinner parties on Friday and Saturday nights. By Sunday afternoon, most of the group owned at least one home site, sometimes more. GDC literature stated the following: "Expert planning to give the home buyer the most for his money is a hallmark of GDC home communities. Mass home building can be done without losing the custom built look. At all GDC communities a particular type of house is assigned to each lot. The homes are spaced well apart for privacy and the assignment plan insures against the monotony of project type construction. GDC does no speculative building and each home has been purchased before construction starts." (Courtesy of Frank E. Mackle III.)

Throughout 1960 and 1961, several areas of disagreement began to arise between the Mackle Company and General Development Corporation. These disagreements resulted in the Mackle Brothers agreeing to be bought out in February 1962. GDC continued to market properties in Port Charlotte. (Courtesy of Charlotte County Historical Center.)

PORT CHARLOTTE *is growing all the time*

Marketing to out-of-state buyers sight-unseen allowed prices to increase unrestrained beyond the local price of identical lots. Meanwhile, Port Charlotte continued to grow. However, the disparity between new and resale prices began to cause problems in the 1970s for GDC. (Courtesy of Carolyn Depenbrock.)

Pictures such as these showing a peaceful, happy suburban lifestyle were distributed in brochures throughout the United States and Europe. The below picture is at the corner of Waltham Street and Dover Avenue, looking south on Dover. In the 1970s, GDC increased its home selling price and offered the lot buyer the option to trade the lot back in as a down payment on a house at the current GDC lot price. As a result, home prices were inflated to cover the potential trade. This worked well into the 1980s but came to an end with the criminal conviction of four GDC personnel. GDC once offered a home priced at between $85,000 and $100,000 as a prize on the *Dream House* game show in the 1980s. The home was later appraised at under $50,000. (Both courtesy of Carolyn Depenbrock.)

The Port Charlotte Beach Complex area was a sparse development in 1961. This picture is looking south toward the Beach Complex. U.S. 41 is in the lower left corner of the picture. Elkcam Boulevard (running north-south) is in the bottom middle of the picture flanked by Port Charlotte Boulevard to the right and Sunrise Trail to the left. Sunrise Trail turns and runs parallel to U.S. 41 at the bottom of the picture, and the four homes seen there in close proximity to each other could be the first model homes built in the area in 1956. (Both courtesy of Charlotte County Historical Center.)

This picture shows the Beach Complex from the Peace River, looking north toward the Port Charlotte development. Note the absence of canals north of the Beach Complex. (Courtesy of Charlotte County Historical Center.)

These pictures are taken from advertisements promoting Port Charlotte. Brochures promoted fishing piers for the enjoyment of new residents. GDC sponsored "Southward Ho" or "SoHo" trips where the company paid for the customer to visit Port Charlotte for a few days. GDC offered its own in-house financing through a company called GDV, which was a wholly owned subsidiary and eventually started prohibiting salespeople from recommending other means of financing. GDV would provide the appraisal, which the customer never saw. The appraised home was compared with other GDC homes that were sold nationally, not those selling in the same area. Salespeople informed customers that if they would keep their homes for a year, the home could be sold at a profit. (Above courtesy of Frank E. Mackle III; right courtesy of Carolyn Depenbrock.)

The pictures on pages 78 and 79 were printed in brochures used to advertise Port Charlotte. A Miami newspaper reported in February 1956 that the Mackle Company was rated ninth in the nation for home builders. The article reported that Mackle home costs ranged between $4,950 for a one-bedroom home to $7,750 for a three-bedroom home. (Courtesy of Carolyn Depenbrock.)

Older "folk" were surveyed about what types of housing they desired. It was reported that they wanted small homes on small lots near the ocean and near recreation centers. They also wanted to be near established communities with shopping centers and public transportation. (Courtesy of Carolyn Depenbrock.)

These pictures appeared in brochures advertising Port Charlotte and the water recreation available to residents. During one week in 1958, the Mackle Company hit an all-time record high in home site sales, totaling $3 million. During that same week, home sites sold in Port Charlotte totaled 1,636. By 1962, there were 3,116 homes in Port Charlotte according to the Census Committee of the Port Charlotte Civic Association. At one point, Frank Mackle Jr. predicted that the Mackle Company would be building homes at the rate of 25,000 each year with 3,900 predicted to be built in Port Charlotte. (Above courtesy of Frank E. Mackle III; below courtesy of Carolyn Depenbrock.)

PORT CHARLOTTE has 40 miles of scenic waterfront including sandy beaches such as this one for exclusive use of the residents. If you enjoy "being near the water," Port Charlotte is made to order for you. Moor your boat in Charlotte Harbor. Take your choice of fresh or salt water fishing: pick the spot where they're biting best.

Now anyone can share in the growth of

FLORIDA'S FABULOUS PORT CHARLOTTE

These pictures appeared in *Life* and *Newsweek* magazines as part of full-page advertisements for the Port Charlotte Development. In the late 1950s and early 1960s, a huge retirement market was expected to impact Florida's growth. Modern trends toward longer life, increased leisure time, earlier retirement, and expanded Social Security and pension funds would allow 9 or 10 million new people to enter the retirement market over a span of five years' time. The Mackle Company predicted that if only five percent of the new retirees decided to come to Florida, it would create a demand for 80,000 to 100,000 new homes each year. (Both courtesy of Frank E. Mackle III.)

These pictures also appeared in brochures advertising Port Charlotte. By 1960, the Port Charlotte Civic Association was seeking the support of Florida members of congress to obtain an independent post office for the community. The civic association met monthly, and Pres. Roy Hogan informed residents that eventually other civic services would be essential to the community. Port Charlotte was being served by a branch of the Punta Gorda Post Office via a substation at the Car and Home Supply Store at 414 Access Road. Other needs identified as a result of growth were street lighting, police and fire departments, a welfare agency, and a disaster squadron. (Left courtesy of Carolyn Depenbrock; below courtesy of Frank E. Mackle III.)

In 1989, some 12,000 customers filed a class-action lawsuit against GDC, alleging misleading sales practices. GDC pled guilty to fraud, filed bankruptcy, and set up a trust fund to reimburse customers through mortgage subsidies. GDC reorganized as Atlantic Gulf Communities. Four GDC upper management personnel were indicted for fraud and conspiracy in connection with GDC home sales between 1982 and 1989: David Brown, Robert Ehrling, Tore DeBella, and Richard Reizen. Brown and Reizen were sentenced to five years each. Ehrling was sentenced to 121 months, and DeBella was sentenced to 97 months. However, in 1996, these sentences were reversed by the U.S. Court of Appeals, citing the fact that GDC never prevented customers from investigating the local housing market themselves to discover how GDC homes compared in local value. (Both courtesy of Carolyn Depenbrock.)

This 75-foot lighthouse replica at Conway Boulevard and U.S. 41 announces free admission to the "Port Charlotte Exhibition of Homes." Advertisements in *Newsweek* and *Life* magazines boasted home sites for as little as $10 down and $10 a month. The first homes, pitched to middle-income retirees, were occupied in October 1956. Hurricane Donna destroyed the tower in 1960. The above picture is looking south on Conway; the area became known as the "Lighthouse District." The picture below comes from an advertising brochure. The early Charlotte Chamber of Commerce shared space with the Charlotte County Sheriff Substation. (Above courtesy of Charlotte County Historical Center; below courtesy of Carolyn Depenbrock.)

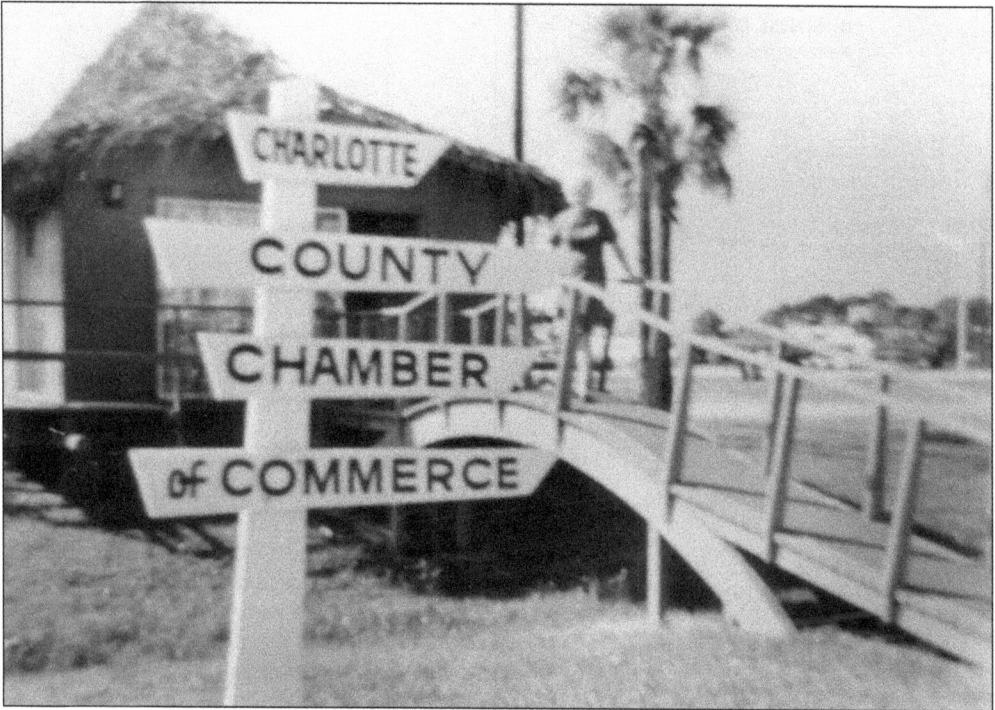

With the development of Port Charlotte in the 1950s, there were so many inquiries about the new area that a Port Charlotte Chamber of Commerce was formed. It occupied a "tiki hut" style building situated on the property that is now the Promenades Mall. The retirement community brought steady financial gains and economic stability to the Florida economy in the late 1950s and early 1960s. It was estimated that residents of General Development communities were pumping $20 million each year into the state's economy. The Charlotte County Chamber of Commerce, Inc., now is a membership association of more than 1,300 businesses and organizations. (Both courtesy of Charlotte County Historical Center.)

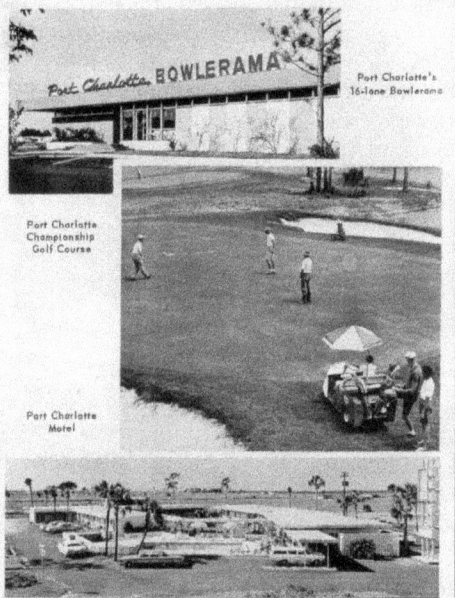

The image at left is from the business directory for the chamber of commerce in 1963. The image below is an advertisement for businesses in the area. In August 1960, television game show host Dennis James and Elliott Mackle, president of the Mackle Company, attended the grand opening of the Port Charlotte Motel, located at Access Road and Elkcam Waterway. The 30-unit motel boasted an ultramodern tropical arrangement, Florida decor furnishings, and a boat dock on Elkcam Waterway. Other amenities included a swimming pool, air-conditioned rooms, carpeting, and individual phones. (Both courtesy of Carolyn Depenbrock.)

The image at right is from the chamber of commerce listing of churches. Below is advertising in a local publication. The year 1960 also saw the construction of a modern 12-lane bowling alley. Charlotte Lanes, located at U.S. 41 and Harbor View Road, was expected to be open in October. Cost for the 10,000-square-foot building was estimated at $300,000. The parking lot was planned to hold a minimum of 200 cars and would provide locker rooms for men and women, a league meeting room, snack shop, and a Brunswick pro store. A light source and electric eye receiver named Tel-E-Foul would detect a bowler's foot crossing the foul line and sound a buzzer. A bowling program for young bowlers was also planned. (Both courtesy of Carolyn Depenbrock.)

First Baptist Church — Peachland Blvd., Port Charlotte

Jewish Community Group — Harriet St., Port Charlotte

The Church of the Brethren — Olean & Conway Blvd., Port Charlotte

Christian and Missionary Alliance — 391 Waltham St., Port Charlotte

The Church of God of Prophecy —

Bible Baptist Church — 185 N.W. Glendale Port Charlotte

Jehovah's Witnesses — Kingdom Hall 706 Hazel St.

Church of Christ — Marion and Brown St.

St. Charles Borromeo Catholic Church — N. Easy Street, Port Charlotte

Port Charlotte Methodist — Viscaya Drive

Port Charlotte Episcopal Mission — Community Center, Easy Street

Peace Chapel of Harbour Heights — Civic Bldg.

North Port Charlotte Methodist Church — North Port Charlotte Community Center

First Baptist Church — Charlotte Harbor

First United Presbyterian Church — Harvey Street

Assembly of God Church — Taylor St. at E. Dr., La Punta Pk.

Community Methodist Church — Cleveland, Florida

Trinity Methodist Church — Charlotte Harbor

Charlotte Drive-In Church Service —

Holy Trinity Lutheran Church — Port Charlotte Community Center

Tee and Green Baptist Mission — Community Center

Church of Jesus Christ of the Latter Day Saints — Community Center, Port Charlotte

Church of Christ — Port Charlotte

Colored Church

Bethel A.M.E. Church —

St. Mark Baptist Church —

Macedonia Baptist Church —

St. Mary Primitive Baptist Church —

Centenary Methodist — Corner Milus and E. Charlotte Ave.

The Church of the Living God — Cor. Charlotte Ave. & Cochran

Port Charlotte's own bank has assets of well over $3,000,000.

New Post Office building at Port Charlotte. Mail is delivered door-to-door.

The spanking-new Port Charlotte "Bowlerama" has 16 lanes.

The photograph at left advertises Port Charlotte Bank (at the corner of Aaron and Olean Streets), Port Charlotte Post Office, and Port Charlotte Bowlerama. Below, in the lower right-hand corner, are the first four houses built on Sunrise Trail. The beginnings of Adams Court can be seen in the horseshoe shape in the picture. U.S. 41 runs along the left of the picture from top to bottom. The area of trees on the left is now the Promenades Mall. This picture was taken in 1957. (Left courtesy of Carolyn Depenbrock; below courtesy of Charlotte County Historical Center.)

The above picture is from 1963, looking southeast toward Punta Gorda. It shows the widening of U.S. 41 with the Promenades Mall on the left. At the time, it was called Port Charlotte Shopping Center and was built by General Development Corporation as part of the development of the city. On the right is the finished Adams Court. The commercial businesses that began to appear along U.S. 41 can be seen in the center. The picture below is an aerial view of the Port Charlotte Shopping Center as it appeared in 1967. (Both courtesy of Charlotte County Historical Center.)

The Port Charlotte Shopping Center opened in January 1960 at the intersection of U.S. 41 and Harbor Boulevard. The plaza became the area's shopping hub in the 1960s with stores such as Meisners 5&10 and Kwik Chek. The shopping center served as a bus terminal for two bus routes with 55 community stops. The buses operated from 8:00 a.m. to 6:00 p.m. Fares were 10¢ one way and 15¢ round-trip with free transfers. The shopping center burned in late 1973 and was replaced by the current Promenades Mall, which opened in 1976. (Above courtesy of Charlotte County Historical Center; below courtesy of Frank E. Mackle III.)

The Port Charlotte Transit Company, a subsidiary of General Development Corporation, received a franchise from the state in 1960 to operate intra-community bus service with two buses holding 20 passengers each. The below picture was used to advertise the amenities that GDC had developed in Port Charlotte so new residents would not have to travel far for necessities. The State Road Department proposed the installation of "pull around" lanes and yellow "no passing" lines at four intersections on U.S. 41 in Port Charlotte in an effort to ease traffic congestion. A "pull around" lane would allow rear-approaching traffic to move around left-turning vehicles. The first improvements were installed at Easy Street and U.S. 41 to test its effect on traffic. (Both courtesy of Carolyn Depenbrock.)

Port Charlotte's first commercial building was a 7-Eleven store located near Waterway Circle. These early-1958 businesses show the beginnings of the development along U.S. 41 and the access roads. The 55-mile-per-hour speed limit on U.S. 41 was being debated by the State Road Department and the Port Charlotte Civic Association. The State Road Department suggested erecting four "congested area" signs and more speed-limit markers. Problem intersections along U.S. 41 were identified as Easy Street, Galway Lane, Harbor Boulevard, and in front of the Port Charlotte Shopping Center. (Both courtesy of Charlotte County Historical Center.)

The above picture shows, from left to right, Robert Mackle, Frank Mackle, and Chi Chi Rodriguez at the grand opening of the Port Charlotte Golf Club. The golf course was originally completed as a nine-hole course; later the back nine holes were added to make it a championship golf course, well over the PGA minimum of 6,600 yards. The par-72 course was planned by General Development Corporation. New innovations planned for the back nine holes included a double fairway on the first hole and a hole divided by trees and shrubbery to make the course more challenging. The image at right shows a frustrated Frank Mackle III searching for a lost golf ball. (Both courtesy of Frank E. Mackle III.)

The Port Charlotte Cultural Center began as the idea of 25 residents who saw a need for a center for adult education and culture. Newcomers to Port Charlotte were having difficulty adjusting to idle time away from family and friends. General Development Corporation donated 3 acres of land in the middle of the rapidly developing residential area. Grant money and local resident contributions provided the funds to build a library, theater, auditorium, and classrooms that opened in 1968. Since then, there have been 11 additions to the center. Eventually, GDC donated more than 8 acres for the expanding project. The Cultural Center became the gathering place for all kinds of social events. Below, Jo Wheeler is recognized for competing in a pinochle party. (Both courtesy of the Cultural Center of Charlotte County.)

The adult education center was formally created by renting a store on Easy Street and hiring a couple of retired teachers to conduct a variety of classes. James Baldwin, a newly retired teacher from Indiana, was put in charge of the center. Thirteen subjects were offered to 250 residents for a registration fee of $2. The first graduation was held in June 1961 for 29 students, whose average age was 64. By 1963, a full 43 courses were being offered with four of them accredited by Edison Junior College. One of the most popular classes was an art class. Another popular class was a nurse's aid class. The classes were referred to as Port Charlotte "U." (Both courtesy of the Cultural Center of Charlotte County.)

Classes continue to be held at the Cultural Center, making it a notable local gathering place for both newcomers and long-term residents. Lectures, shows, and expositions are regularly held as the Cultural Center partners with institutions such as the chamber of commerce and local hospitals to bring information to residents. Computer classes, card games, and workshops are also offered. Hundreds of volunteers make the Cultural Center thrive. The center contains a cafeteria, a gym, a resale shop, and various meeting rooms. Classes offered include wood carving, quilting, clogging, art, and music. (Both courtesy of the Cultural Center of Charlotte County.)

This postcard (front and back) shows St. Joseph Hospital and the surrounding area. This view is looking at the hospital from Harbor Boulevard with the Elkcam Waterway shown behind the hospital. The postcard boasts a 6¢ Eisenhower stamp. The postcard reads, "Here is a new part of Charlotte County. Pop had never seen it. He would be surprised. This is across the harbor from Punta Gorda." By 1962, Port Charlotte's retiree population had grown so large that the lone hospital in Punta Gorda could not support the medical needs of these residents. (Both courtesy of Joan Ehrman.)

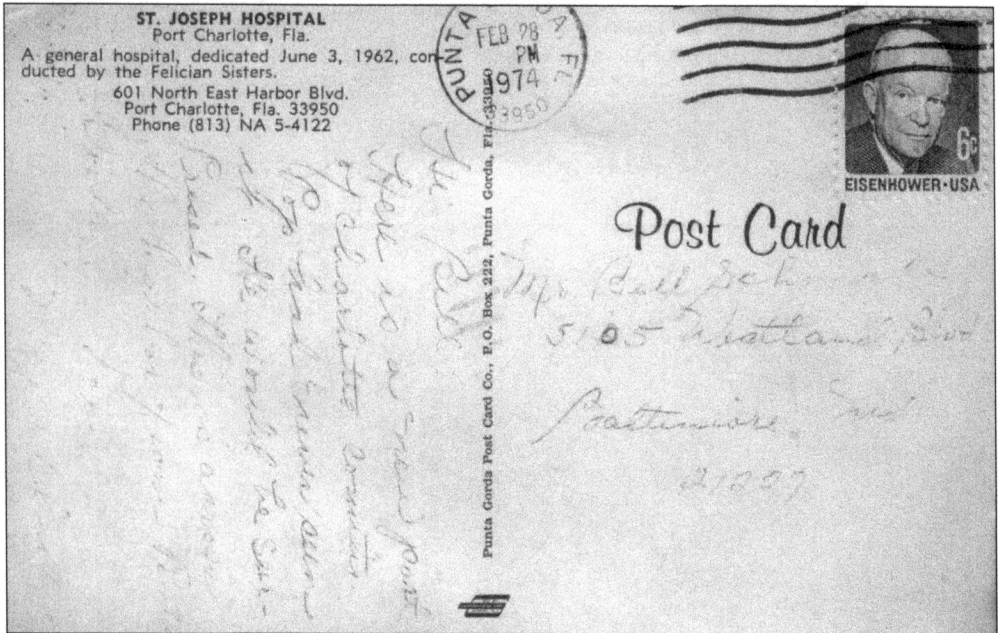

Peace River Regional Medical Center opened in 1962 as St. Joseph Hospital and was established by the Felician Sisters. Over 1,000 Port Charlotte residents attended the groundbreaking ceremonies on June 19, 1960. Construction of the $1 million facility was delayed because of lack of funds and changes in the plans. There were three full-time physicians and one part-time physician when it opened with 50 patient beds. The population of Port Charlotte was reported by the Census Committee of the Civic Association at 6,913, with 1,314 of those under the age of 18. (Both courtesy of Peace River Regional Medical Center.)

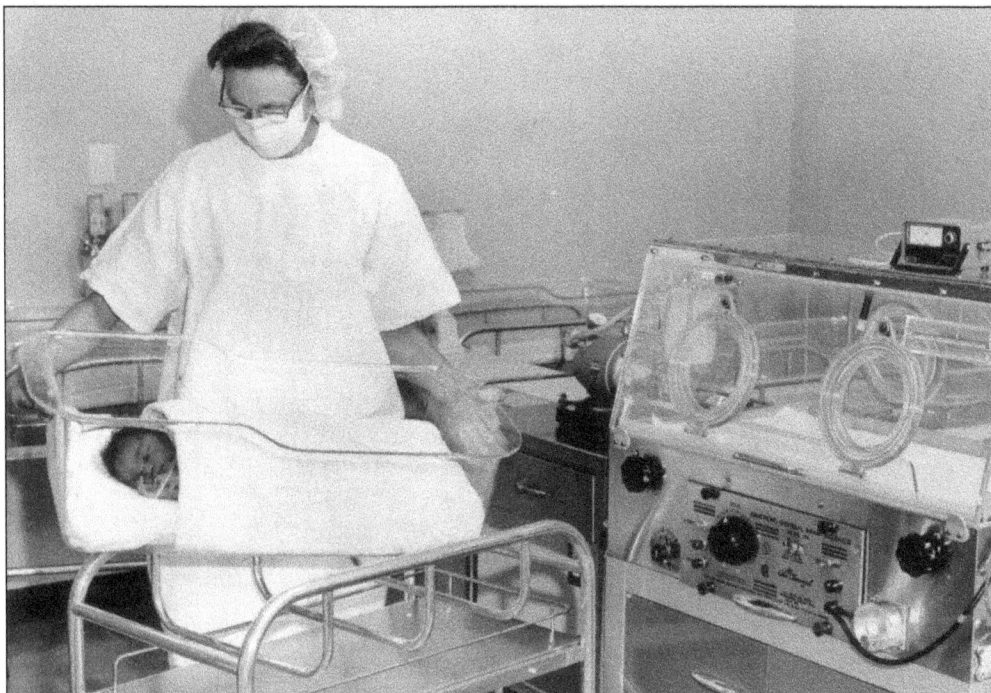

The photograph above shows Nurse Mary Tollett in the newborn nursery. In the picture at right, Nurse Evalyn Turley demonstrates the performance of a brain scan in 1962 on Mary Snow in the nuclear medicine department. A typical brain scan in the early 1960s was performed by draining cerebrospinal fluid and replacing it with air, then performing an x-ray to see the brain structure. This procedure was performed extensively until it was deemed to be too dangerous. By the late 1980s, it was largely abandoned by the medical community. Modern MRI and CAT scans have replaced this early technology. (Both courtesy of Peace River Regional Medical Center.)

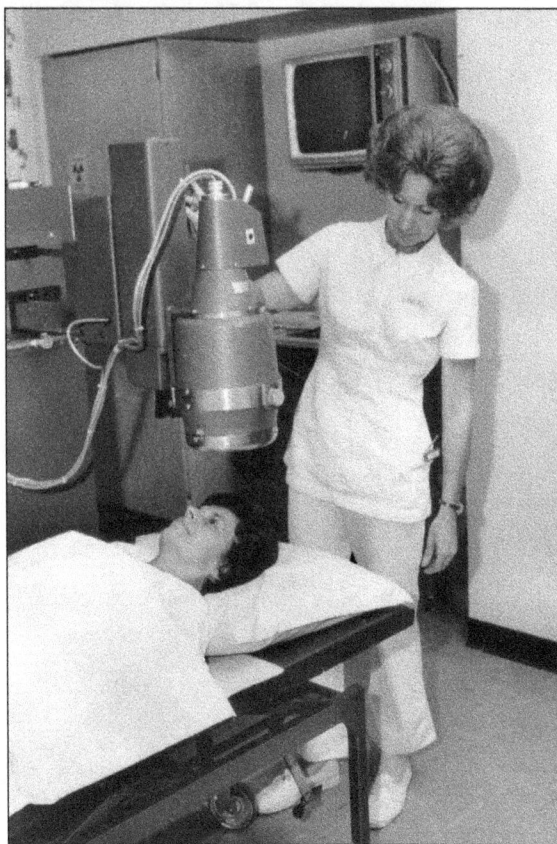

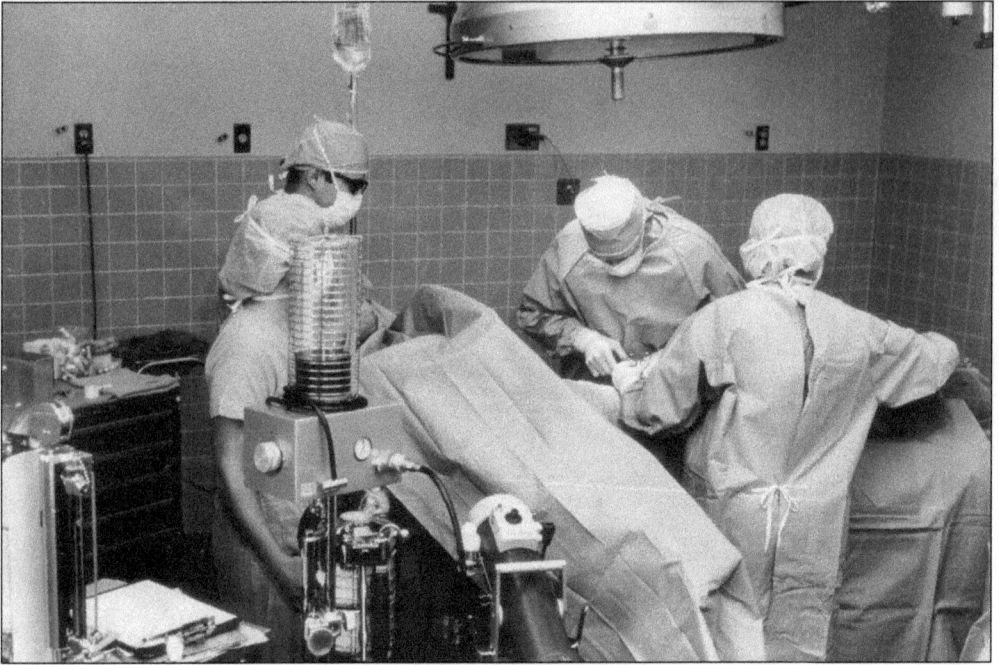

When St. Joseph Hospital opened, it had an outpatient clinic, pharmacy, maternity section, x-ray department, and lab facilities. The below picture shows, from left to right, Dr. Fred Swing, Dr. Eugene McLaughlin, Sister Augustine, and Dr. Alfonso Annicchiarico in the staff conference room. Plans called for adding a 50-bed nursing home and a modern operating room. By 1975, the hospital had grown to 212 beds and was renamed Bon Secours–St. Joseph Hospital in 1987 after the Felician and Bon Secours communities began collaborative efforts. The name was officially changed to Peace River Regional Medical Center in 2005. (Both courtesy of Peace River Regional Medical Center.)

The above photograph is of the dietary department of the annex, which was the patient care area. The annex later became the nursing home. In photograph below, Grace Johnson and Evelyn and Mike Miskanic are shown in the hospital's cafeteria. After the initial ground-breaking in June 1960, construction had been restricted to just the four walls of the one-story structure for months. A change in plans that needed to be approved in Jacksonville as well as a lack of funds caused construction delays. Fund-raising activities were held to allow work to continue on the million-dollar facility. (Both courtesy of Peace River Regional Medical Center.)

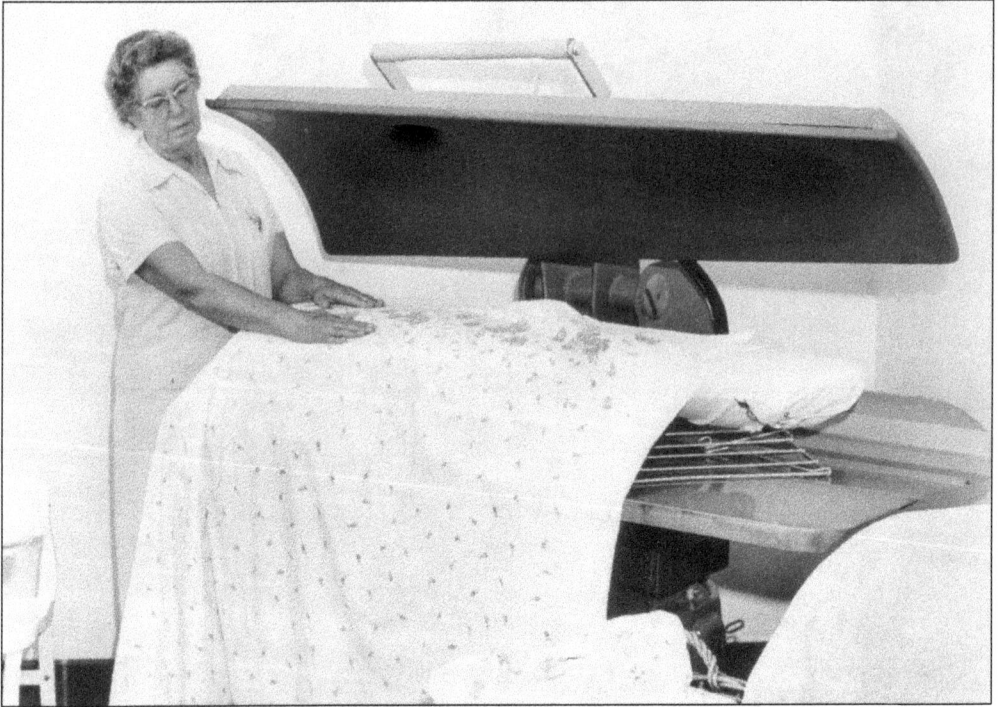

The hospital was built by General Development Corporation for the Catholic Church. Approximately 75 workers built the structure, which was advertised to have both private and semi-private rooms. The above picture shows Bonnie Kopriver operating the press mangle, a mechanical laundry aid used to press sheets. In later years, modern laundry dryers eliminated the need to press sheets. The laundry is now located in the nursing home. At left, Warren Barnett operates the multilith machine in the print shop of the hospital. A multilith machine is equivalent to a printing press. The print shop was closed in the 1990s. (Both courtesy of Peace River Regional Medical Center.)

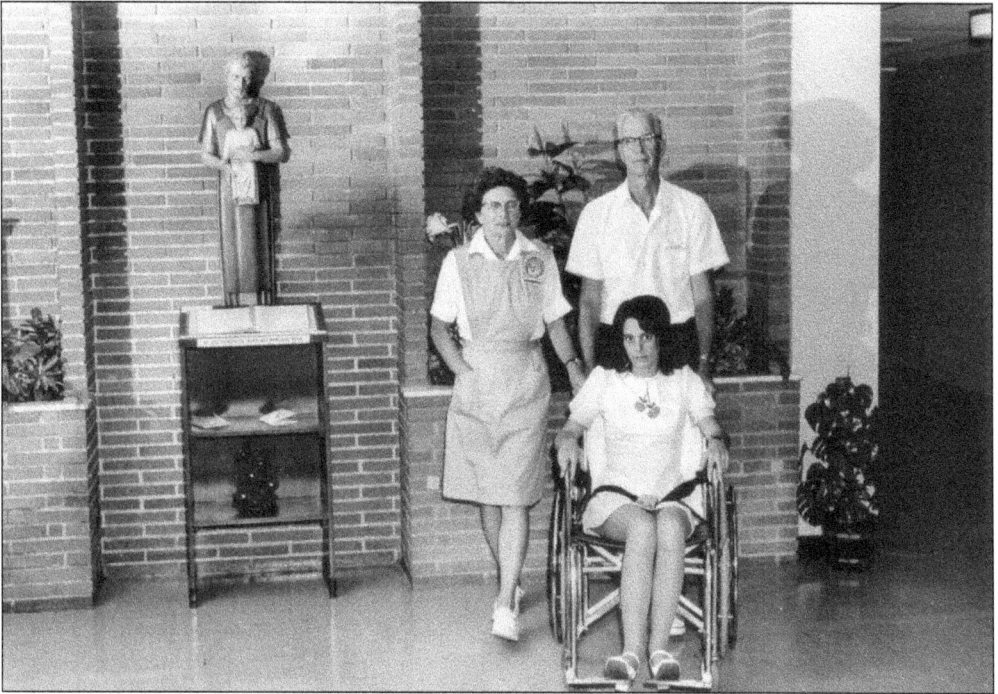

Above are "Pink Lady" Mrs. Booth and Mac Booth assisting patient Patricia Crenshaw as she is discharged from the hospital. "Pink Lady" is another term for hospital volunteer. Peace River has a staff of over 300 volunteers who donate thousands of service hours each year. The picture below shows the modernization of the hospital seen in the construction of this "patient tower," completed in 1984. Each year for the past four years, Peace River Regional has received the HealthGrades' Distinguished Hospital Award for Clinical Excellence. In 2007, they were awarded the Maternity Care Excellence Award and the Distinguished Hospital Award for Patient Safety. (Both courtesy of Peace River Regional Medical Center.)

This is the ground-breaking for the Bon Secours physician office building, also called the Medical Arts building. Peace River Regional Medical Center has undergone many changes over the years. The current orthopedic wing was originally the pediatric unit. Updated x-ray and respiratory departments were completed in 1977. A modernized operating room and day surgery unit was completed in 1992. The emergency room was renovated in 2003 and the neonatal intensive care unit added in 2008. Originally, Sister Kathleen of the St. Joseph's Order in Baden, Pennsylvania, was the hospital administrator. She had previously worked at St. Joseph's Hospital in Pittsburgh. (Both courtesy of Peace River Regional Medical Center.)

Five

LATE 20TH CENTURY

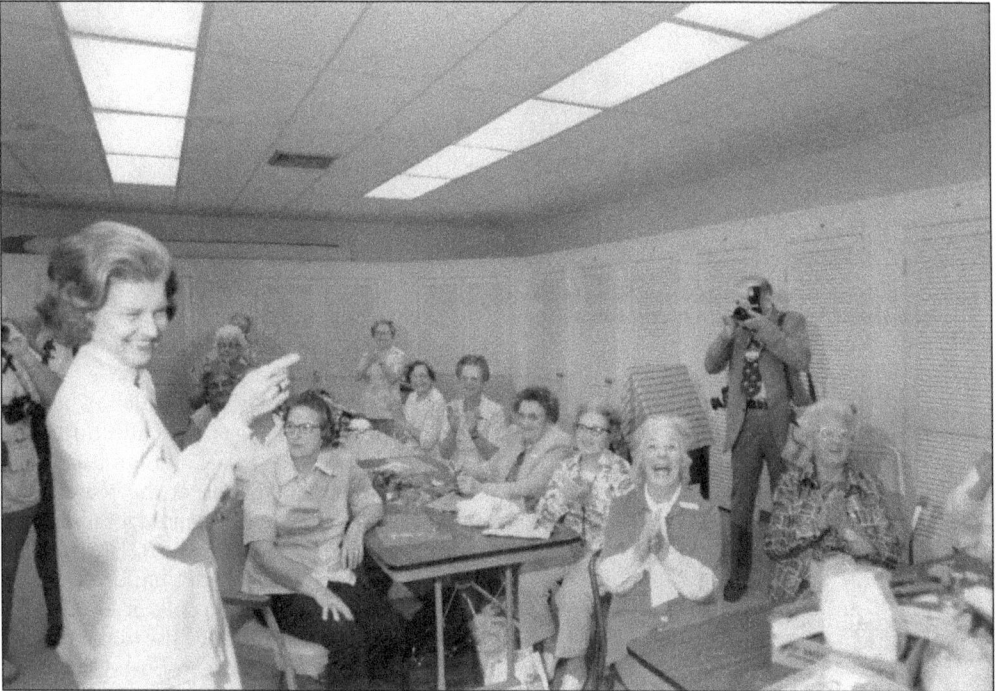

In February 1976, Betty Ford visited the Cultural Center. During her 90-minute visit, she spoke to a cancer survivor group about her experience with breast cancer. It was her first solo campaign trip to garner support for Pres. Gerald Ford in the upcoming March primary against Ronald Reagan. Floyd Pfeiffer, president of the Adult Education Association, had written to every president since President Johnson, asking them to visit the Cultural Center to see an example of people taking responsibility for themselves rather than asking government to help them. The official response from the White House was that this visit was to honor the group of people who made the Cultural Center a reality and give the Cultural Center the national attention it deserved. (Courtesy of the Cultural Center of Charlotte County.)

BARBARA BUSH

September 4, 1992

Dear Port Charlotte Cultural Center
Staff and Residents,

So many thanks for such a
lovely afternoon. I loved my visit
with you all. The clown is adorable
and the beautiful card with the
thoughtful inscription will be a
special reminder of a wonderful day.

Both George and I truly
appreciate your support.

With all best wishes,

Warmly,

Barbara Bush

We loved our visit. Thank
you!

In October 1992, Barbara Bush visited the Cultural Center, had lunch, and spoke to about 250 people in the Centennial Room of the Cultural Center. She is pictured here with Dee McDaniels, who has been volunteering at the Cultural Center for over 20 years. Later on, Bush spoke to about 300 people at the Murdock Carrousel Mall who had waited for about two hours in the rain to see her. During her 45-minute visit to Port Charlotte, she made some campaign calls at GOP headquarters in advance of the upcoming November election between Bush-Quayle and Clinton-Gore. (Both courtesy of the Cultural Center of Charlotte County.)

The above picture shows concert master James Zhang on the first row in the forefront. Linda Salisbury is in the forefront below. The Charlotte Symphony Orchestra is in its 30th season. The performance pictured here is the first concert at the Edison College's Charlotte campus in May 1997. Performances are held at the Charlotte Performing Arts Center and at the new Charlotte Harbor Event Center. In addition to the Charlotte Symphony, other musical groups in the area in the 1990s included the Charlotte County Cultural Center Community Chorus, the Charlotte Chorale, the Community Handbell Choir of Port Charlotte, and the Charlotte County Recorder Ensemble. (Both courtesy of Charlotte Symphony Orchestra.)

The Cultural Center was the first home of the Charlotte Symphony. The Charlotte Players also began performing at the auditorium of the Cultural Center. The above picture was taken at a 1980s performance of the symphony. The photograph at left is of two young musicians who participated in the youth symphony through a summer school program. Janita Hauk was Charlotte Symphony's musical director in the 1990s. When the symphony performed at the Cultural Center, Ruth Scherer would give a 30-minute pre-concert lecture about music appreciation. Ruth had previously given music appreciation lectures with the Cleveland Orchestra and Detroit Symphony. (Both courtesy of Charlotte Symphony Orchestra.)

The Charlotte County school system began with the first school in Charlotte Harbor Town in 1873. The school system was then part of Manatee County's school system and had nine free schools totaling 200 white pupils. Between 1960 and 2000, a total of 17 new schools were built to handle the rapid growth. Port Charlotte High School was one of those new schools. It opened its doors in 1982. The below picture shows, from left to right, school senators Chris Beisner, Susan Sorrentino, Jerry Cohee, Debbie Peevey, Todd Nichols, Jeff Murray, Stacy Skinner, Debbie Cravey, Tracy Herman, Brian Riley, and Pam Blake. (Both courtesy of Port Charlotte High School.)

In 1921, Charlotte County was carved out of DeSoto County and W. E. Bell was appointed the first superintendent. He complained that he had inherited an $8,500 deficit from the DeSoto County school system and in 1924 recommended that students who failed to comply with the compulsory attendance law be jailed. Construction of the first bridge allowed students to be bused from the rural communities to the junior high at Charlotte Harbor that had been built in 1917. Six buses operated on a budget of $30 per student per semester. These pictures show workmen building Port Charlotte High School, Charlotte County's third high school. Lemon Bay High School had been constructed in 1962. (Both courtesy of Port Charlotte High School.)

By 1926, the average salary for a Florida teacher was $615 a year for teachers who taught in a two-room school, $766 a year in schools of 3–10 rooms, and $933 a year for teachers in a school of 10-plus rooms. Charlotte County teacher salaries were the highest in the state. They earned $1,000 a year if they taught in a one-room school and $1,200 a year if they taught in a two-room school. During the Depression, the school year was reduced to seven months and teachers received promissory notes for food and clothing from local stores rather than a paycheck. The above picture shows construction of Port Charlotte High School. Below is an advertisement that appeared in the school's first yearbook in 1982. (Both courtesy of Port Charlotte High School.)

Pictured here is the 1982 Port Charlotte High School football team. From left to right are (first row) Tim Frank, Billy Howarth, Keith Locker, Joe Tiseo, John Possel, Dave Burstrom, Jeff Filkins, Ken White, Cal DeMier, Merv Samuels, Richard Bartch, Tim Hornish, Jerry Mazzoni, and Henderson McCullough; (second row) Brett Popovich, Michael Schaefer, Darren Cummings, Jeff Vargo, Mark Priselac, Jack Renna, Steve Demay, cocaptain Richie Booher, Brett Wilder, Bobby Dunn, David Anthony, Anthony Sciarretta, Brian Hernandez, and Don Lutinski; (third row) cocaptain Bob Bruglio, Tom Brioc, Brian Hoffman, Dan Kinney, Brian O'Neil, Bryan MeGill, Carmine Feola, Andy DuBois, Paul Heerman, Chris Johnson, Jack Riggs, Chuck Swinamer, and Scott Amick. (Both courtesy of Port Charlotte High School.)

Pictured here is the cheerleading squad from Port Charlotte High School's 1982 yearbook: (first row) Sam Blake and Lynda Schrage; (second row) Krista Doxie and Marnie White; (third row) Joy Davis, Monica Shirley, Raegen Jones, and Stef Thomsen; (fourth row) Lisa Nisi, Lauren Larkin, and Jennifer Fitzgerald; (fifth row) Tracey Herman, Carol Possel, and Missy Cummins. (Courtesy of Port Charlotte High School.)

The 1982 girls' junior varsity basketball team at Port Charlotte High School included, from left to right, (first row) Verra Kosturi, Karen Powers, Kim O'Connell, Karen Camble, Debbie Miller, and Elaine Ponzio; (second row) Coach Barbara Beckham, Sue Pipler, Pam Ridolfi, Charmaine Samuels, Debbie Nease, Stacy DeWeaver, and Pam Blake. (Courtesy of Port Charlotte High School.)

Pictured here is the boys' junior varsity basketball team from Port Charlotte High School. They are, from left to right, (first row) John Whaley, Scott Amick, Jeff Dudley, and Bob Harrison; (second row) assistant coach Don Wendell, manager Kevin Enwright, Brian Shriner, Richard Boysen, Scott Barber, Lou Candelaria, Tim Hornish, manager Keith Enwright, and Coach James Dean. (Courtesy of Port Charlotte High School.)

Members of the 1982 girls' varsity volleyball team from Port Charlotte High School are, from left to right, (first row) captain Michele Noel, Traci Ainscough, Sam Blake, and Angela Pereira; (second row) Selina Nickerson, Cheryl Kern, Pam Blake, Pam Ridolfi, Charmaine Samuels, and Beth Walker. (Courtesy of Port Charlotte High School.)

This picture is of students at Charlotte Harbor School, the district's school for children with special needs. Before the school was opened in 1980, Charlotte County's special needs children were sent to DeSoto County for schooling. Special education is handled differently in each local school district. (Courtesy of Charlotte Harbor School.)

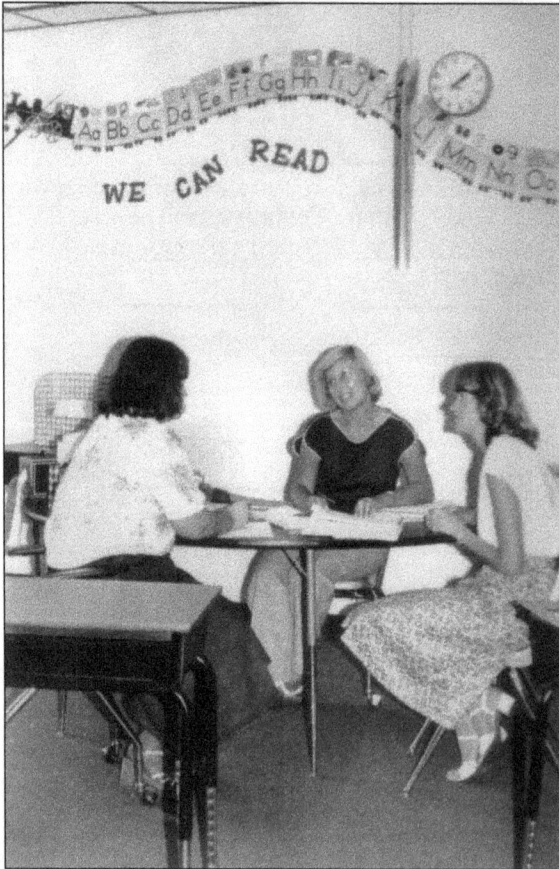

The above picture shows teacher Mary Morgan receiving a funding check in the early days of Charlotte Harbor School. On the left is the school's director, Bill Byrd. The photograph at left shows, from left to right, teachers Laura Allen, Mary Morgan, and Kathy Draeger. Students with special needs receive education in a variety of ways, including segregation, mainstreaming, or inclusion. The Individuals with Disabilities Education Act requires school districts to include students with special needs in regular education activities as much as possible. However, some parents prefer to have their children attend a special needs school. Until the passage of the Education for All Handicapped Children Act in 1975, American schools educated only one-fifth of children with disabilities. More than one million students were refused access to public schools. (Both courtesy of Charlotte Harbor School.)

This picture shows teachers Sue Shoup (left) and Caroline Miller (right) preparing for classes at the newly opened Charlotte Harbor School. In the 1950s and 1960s, families began advocating for the rights of children with disabilities. The federal government passed laws that provided training for teachers. Several landmark court decisions in 1971 and 1972 established the responsibility of states to educate children with disabilities. (Courtesy of Charlotte Harbor School.)

Before 1981, small fire districts existed in Charlotte County that served specific areas. The Charlotte County Fire Service was created by consolidating the East Charlotte Fire Control District and the Alligator Creek Fire District. This picture shows Bill Tursellino on the left and Glenn Taylor on the right. These men are credited with creating Charlotte County's current EMS program. (Courtesy of Charlotte County Fire/EMS.)

In 1986, the county consolidated fire services further, combining the Charlotte County Fire Service (stations Nos. 6 and 7) with the Port Charlotte/Charlotte Harbor Fire Control District (station No. 1) and the Charlotte South Fire Control District (station No. 5), two state fire districts. The name was then changed to the Charlotte County Fire Rescue Department. The picture at right shows Chief Robert Lani, who was the first fire chief in Charlotte County. He served in that capacity for 10 years. The below picture shows Chris Searfoss. She served as Chief Lani's secretary. Both pictures were taken in the 1980s at the old EMS headquarters on Edgewater Drive. (Both courtesy of Charlotte County Fire/EMS.)

Before 1981, emergency medical services were provided by the Charlotte County Sheriff's Office. Ambulance personnel functioned as both a deputy and emergency medical technician. They patrolled in the ambulance but could also write traffic tickets. They were allowed to take the ambulances home at night in case an emergency arose. The ambulance personnel relied heavily on the public to assist in emergencies. Battalion chief Michael Kehoe is shown above, and paramedic Manon Lessard is shown in the picture below. Both pictures are at the old EMS headquarters on Edgewater Drive. The board on the wall behind Paramedic Lessard is a board used to track employee vacations and time off. These pictures were taken in 1992. (Both courtesy of Charlotte County Fire/EMS.)

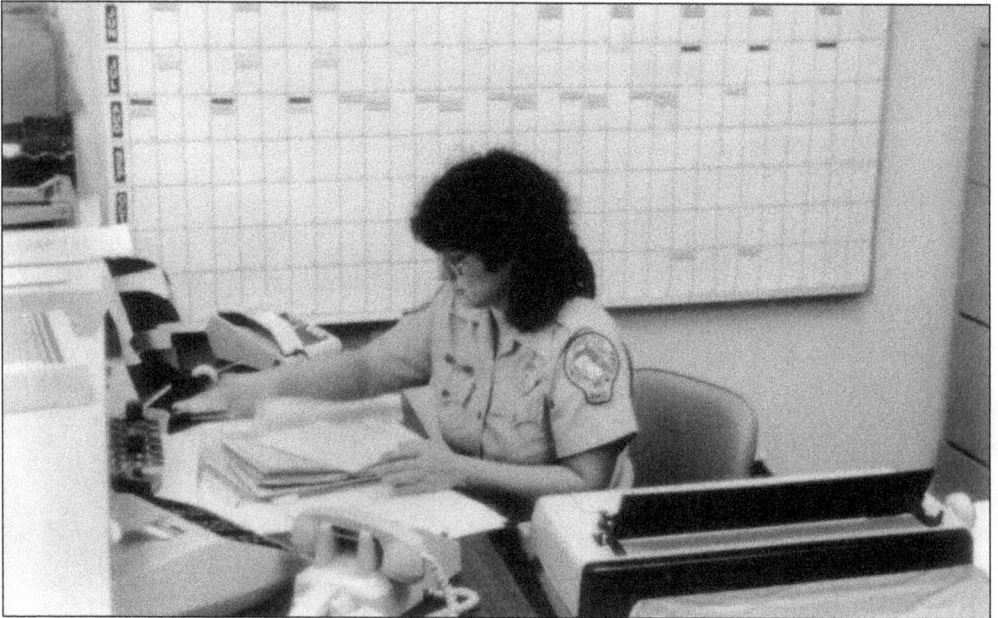

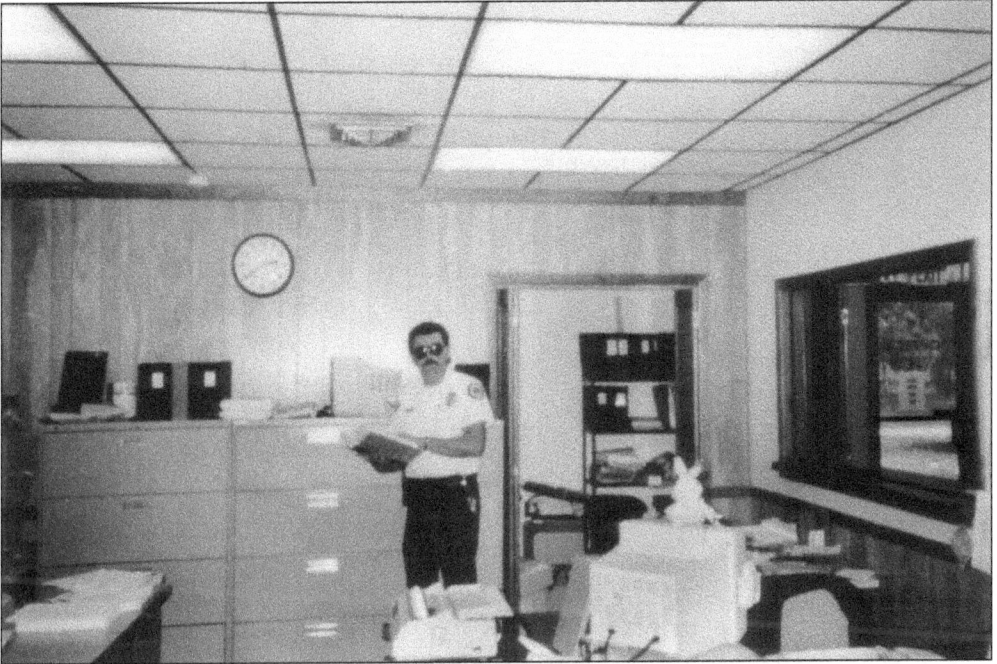

Battalion chief Mike Schulze is shown above at the Edgewater Drive EMS headquarters. The picture below was taken at the annual Emergency Management Service awards banquet held in May. In the late 1980s, training captain Ed Eastman (far right) suffered a heart attack on the job. The four men pictured here, from left to right, firefighter/EMT David Mahon, firefighter/EMT Joseph Madison, fire medic Jay Sanders, and Lt. Billy Cox saved Eastman's life. Mahon received the Phoenix Award, Eastman received Medic of the Year, Cox received Firefighter of the Year, and Sanders received EMT of the year. (Both courtesy of Charlotte County Fire/EMS.)

In 1981, the county created Charlotte County Emergency Medical Services. A fleet of three ambulances provided basic life support services from the Myakka River to the Lee County line. Advanced Life Support was introduced in 1982. In 1983, the fleet was expanded to six units to cover the entire county when the area north of the Myakka River to the Sarasota County line was taken over from Englewood Fire District. In the picture above, fire equipment and other apparatus are being demonstrated at the Port Charlotte Town Center in the late 1980s. In the below picture, firefighter/EMT Jeffrey Mendel (left) and Lt. Thomas Crocker (right) are talking with students at East Elementary School. (Both courtesy of Charlotte County Fire/EMS.)

In 1994, the county combined both fire and emergency medical services into one department, which is now the Charlotte County Fire/EMS. Public outreach, especially to schoolchildren, has become a large part of the job for emergency personnel. At right, fire medic Jeffrey Ehle shows a group of students how emergency personnel deal with emergency medical situations. The below photograph shows fire boat training for the marine unit. Firefighter/EMT Thomas Franz is holding the fire hose nozzle. Other personnel in the photograph are believed to be battalion chief Jon Miller, fire medic Edward Stepp, and fire medic William McClafferty. (Both courtesy of Charlotte County Fire/EMS.)

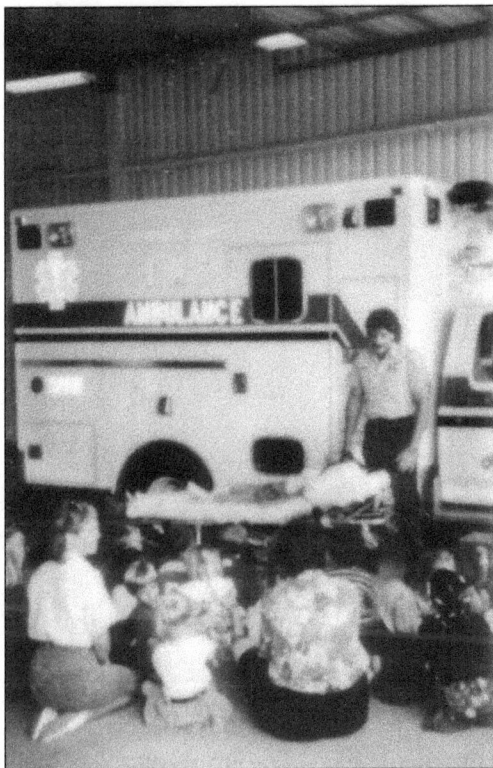

Part of the allure of Port Charlotte for residents who make this their home, whether long or short term, is the proximity to the water. The above picture shows the bridge and pier across the Peace River in the 1960s. The image below shows all three bridges as they existed in 1976. From left to right are the Gilchrist Bridge that was completed in 1976, the Barron Collier Bridge built in 1931, and the original Charlotte Harbor Bridge built in 1921 that was used as a fishing pier. (Above courtesy of Joan Ehrman; below courtesy of Charlotte County Historical Center.)

BIBLIOGRAPHY

Charlotte County Landmarks. Punta Gorda, FL: Stephens/Lane and Associates, 1979.

Robertson, Jim. *At the Cultural Center.* Charlotte Harbor, FL: Tabby House, 1996.

Williams, Lindsey, and U. S. Cleveland. *Our Fascinating Past Charlotte Harbor: Early Years.* Punta Gorda, FL: self-published, 2005.

———. *Our Fascinating Past Charlotte Harbor: The Later Years.* Punta Gorda, FL: Charlotte Harbor Area Historical Society, 1996.

Visit us at
arcadiapublishing.com

www.ingramcontent.com/pod-product-compliance
Lightning Source LLC
Chambersburg PA
CBHW050657150426
42813CB00055B/2212